COMMON CORE STATE STANDARDS FOR LITERACY SERIES
A series designed to help educators successfully implement
CCSS literacy standards in K–12 classrooms

All About Words
Increasing Vocabulary in the Common Core Classroom, PreK–2
Susan B. Neuman and **Tanya Wright**

—UPCOMING IN THIS SERIES—

**Making Literacy a Tool for Disciplinary Learning
in the Common Core Classroom, K–8**
Cynthia L. Brock, Virginia J. Goatley, Taffy E. Raphael,
Catherine M. Weber, and Elisabeth Trost-Shahata

D0840475

All About Words

Increasing Vocabulary in the Common Core Classroom, PreK–2

Susan B. Neuman
Tanya S. Wright

Foreword by Timothy Shanahan

Teachers College, Columbia University
New York and London

Published by Teachers College Press, 1234 Amsterdam Avenue, New York, NY 10027

Library of Congress Cataloging-in-Publication Data

Neuman, Susan B.
  All about words : increasing vocabulary in the common core classroom, prek–2 / Susan B. Neuman and Tanya S. Wright.
    pages cm.
  Includes bibliographical references and index.
  ISBN 978-0-8077-5444-3 (pbk. : alk. paper)—ISBN 978-0-8077-5445-0 (hardcover : alk. paper)
    1. Language arts (Early childhood)   2. Language arts (Early childhood)—Standards.   3. Vocabulary—Study and teaching (Early childhood)   4. Vocabulary—Study and teaching (Early childhood)—Standards.   I. Wright, Tanya S.   II. Title.
LB1139.5.L35N477 2013
372.6—dc23   2013000527

ISBN 978-0-8077-5444-3 (paper)
ISBN 978-0-8077-5445-0 (hardcover)

Printed on acid-free paper
Manufactured in the United States of America

20   19   18   17   16   15   14   13   8   7   6   5   4   3   2   1

Contents

Foreword

I'm starting to write this Foreword sitting in a hotel room with the television keeping me company. *The People's Court* is on, not a favorite show, but I'm starting to make some progress now and don't want to get up and switch stations. But as my attention vacillates between the importance of vocabulary instruction and the legal proceedings on the tube, I'm surprised to find that they are both on the same wavelength.

In the legal case, a couple is suing a caterer for lousy wedding reception service. The caterer explains patiently to the judge that he had to cook the chicken ahead of time because of "clementine weather." It took the judge a few moments and a series of questions to figure out that the caterer meant "inclement" weather. Turns out his vocabulary error even ended up in the contract; not only did the judge laugh at him, but it was a costly error. Words matter.

Ask 1st-graders what makes reading hard and they'll tell you, "the words." Usually when they say that, they are referring to the decoding challenges; but, in fact, long after they can "read" the words, the words' meanings may continue to trip them up. And, like the caterer on television, they aren't always aware that they don't know what the words mean. (I have two daughters, Erin and Meagan. When Meagan was little she was exasperated that, as she put it, "We always run Erins, not Meagans." Think about it.)

Apparently it isn't just the 1st-graders who miss the importance of word meanings in reading. Many instructional programs purport to address early vocabulary teaching, but instead emphasize words that are clearly chosen because of decodability, rather than expanding the children's collection of word meanings.

What results from such oversight and neglect? Clementine weather... but multiplied across hundreds of language interactions every day.

Now that 46 states have adopted the Common Core State Standards, our educational landscape is changing. The Common Core is pushing for major modifications in educational practices: the use of more challenging texts, in terms of reading levels, in grades 2 and up; emphasis on close—or deep or critical—reading and listening; greater attention to the reading of informational texts; more writing about what we read.

Susan Neuman and Tanya Wright's *All About Words* couldn't have come at a better time. If children are going to be engaged successfully in the types of meaning-making envisioned by the Common Core, teachers will need to provide a rich repertoire of supports for children's vocabulary learning—supports consistent with and relevant to the new standards. This practical book is carefully crafted to provide both a research-based consideration of the vocabulary teaching problem, and lots of practical insights into how to teach and otherwise expand children's early language development, especially with informational texts.

I started this Foreword by noting how important words are, but perhaps I exaggerated. Words are only part of the equation; the most important part is the rich meaning and experience underlying words. Words only matter because they serve as a kind of searchable index of ideas, allowing us to connect our new experiences with the information in our minds.

Classrooms that emphasize words—word lists, charts, lessons on isolated word teaching, and so on—can only get you so far. *All About Words* emphasizes the importance of teaching words within a rich context of learning, interpretation, and meaning-making. That's why there is so much here regarding science and social studies ideas (it isn't just literature that matters with young children). If students are going to learn words, they need to learn words that index the experiences relevant to making sense of our social and natural world.

Happy reading, and watch out for clementine weather. It may help to have an umbrella handy because I've noticed that when it's clementine, it usually rains, too.

—Timothy Shanahan,
University of Illinois at Chicago

Preface

We are at an exciting moment in our history of educating young children, preK through grade 2. As a result of a tremendous momentum to ensure that every child receives a high-quality education, states and their school districts all across the United States have adopted new Common Core State Standards in English Language Arts. Together, these standards represent the culmination of an extended, broad-based effort to identify the skills and understandings children will need to become career- and college-ready young adults in the 21st century.

For those of us who work with young children, there's not a moment to wait. Recent evidence from the National Assessment of Educational Progress (NAEP) reports stark achievement gaps in vocabulary across racial and ethnic groups, as well as across income levels. The early years of a child's life provide us with a critical opportunity. It is in these formative years that children come to develop not only the skills but the dispositions to learn—the curiosity, motivation, and eagerness to explore their worlds. It is in these years that children will develop the habits of mind about learning that drive their further development—their desire to know more and their ability to be open to other perspectives and cultures, to value new ideas, and to participate with others constructively in communities of practice. And it is in these years that children will begin to develop the critical communication skills—speaking, listening, reading, and writing—that enable them to convey what they are learning and thinking to others.

It is for these reasons that the Common Core State Standards in English Language Arts are of such relevance to us all. Recently, instruction in the early years of schooling has become too focused on the rudiments of early literacy development. Although all of us recognize that children must learn letters, sounds, and the basic concepts of print, we have often seen a pendulum-swing that has gone too far in one direction. Opportunities for children to engage in rich conversations and discussions of ideas, which are central to oral language development and content learning, have been ignored or, even worse, totally eliminated in some programs. Efforts to engage children in projects and interesting topics with time for individually chosen activities too often have lost out to the teaching of those topics that can be immediately tested or checked using some basic measure.

Common Core State Standards fundamentally change this scenario. These Standards rightfully recognize that literacy is about learning through text. Children need both alphabetic skills and content-rich language opportunities. These Standards are not merely tweaking existing models of how we teach English Language Arts. Rather, they are calling for a sea change—a key shift in the way we think about reading and writing. In essence, they ask us to focus on fewer standards, but with greater depth of understanding than before. These key shifts include:

- **A focus on complexity.** Right from the beginning in preK and kindergarten, teachers are encouraged to engage children in complex texts and the academic language that is associated with the discipline. To read or listen with comprehension, children will need to know the academic terms in science, social studies, math, and the arts, as well as the supporting words, such as *compare* and *contrast, similarity* and *difference,* that can help them talk about these terms and create a shared language for children in classrooms.
- **Evidence.** Reading, writing, speaking, and listening are grounded in evidence from texts, both literary and informational. Rather than rely on background knowledge alone, children will be asked to provide evidence for their understanding. This is an important focus that places more emphasis on questions such as "how do you know?" or "what is in the story that makes you believe this?" Children will have to learn to substantiate their claims, which can lead to better comprehension and higher-level inferences.
- **Knowledge-building through content-rich texts.** A critical feature throughout the Standards, the Common Core focuses on building knowledge through texts. In some cases, this focus has been interpreted as merely greater attention to nonfiction or informational texts. We think it means more than that. It reflects the goals of reading and writing. It means that reading and writing should not only become enjoyable activities, but ones that also build strong content knowledge.

It suggests that texts should be selected purposefully, with the intention of developing both general knowledge and discipline-specific expertise.

At the very center of these important shifts in English Language Arts is language, and the rich vocabulary that will be necessary to meet these new expectations. In some respect, it is *the* gateway to the standards: Without words, children will not able to read complex texts with comprehension or provide evidence from text. They will not be able to comprehend, much less critique, what an author or a speaker has to say, or respond to the veracity of claims or the soundness of someone's reasoning. Put simply, without words it will be difficult for children to participate in developing the capacities to achieve the high expectations of the Common Core.

This is the reason we wrote this book. Recognizing that vocabulary—the ability to understand, use, and organize words and concepts—could represent a major stumbling block for many of our young learners, it becomes even more imperative to provide children with these critical skills early on. This will require powerful instruction that not only improves children's vocabulary, but actually accelerates it, giving them the tools that they will need for meeting these rigorous Common Core Standards. And here's the good news: We know how to do it.

This book is designed to be a highly practical guide for teaching content-rich vocabulary to young children. It is based on years of research with children, teaching them and in turn learning from them. Throughout our work, what has become clear is a simple principle: Children learn when they are taught through meaningful instruction. Even at a young age, they are amazingly capable of discerning authentic inquiry from frivolous activities. They are not fooled easily, and we must not underestimate them.

As you'll see throughout the book, our approach is to describe each aspect of a content-rich vocabulary program, and the decisions that teachers make in planning, presenting, and monitoring the progress of children's word learning. The approach is appropriate for most grades, although we have targeted our efforts to the critical preK through grade 2 years. We start in Chapter 1 by providing a rationale for content-rich vocabulary instruction, building a case for placing greater attention on the intentional development of these skills. We then move in Chapter 2 to a description of the environment.

Although environment cannot on its own teach vocabulary, it can support its development by ensuring easy access to print resources and enhancing verbal interactions within classrooms. Chapter 3 sets out an instructional regime that, as we have seen throughout our work, promotes both vocabulary development and a self-learning device that enables children to begin to build a content-rich vocabulary independently. Although high-quality instruction in vocabulary throughout the grades is essential, at the same time, it is imperative that students learn on their own.

Chapter 4 adds a critical component to our instructional program: the use of materials in ways that begin to scaffold children's understanding of the genre features of literary and informational text. It is our contention that, particularly in the early years, learning has an important affective component. Children need to connect what they're learning with something they care about. Using text sets, we engage children in learning content-specific words in stories, poems, rhymes, and informational books. In Chapter 5, we describe how the management and organization of the classroom can work to your advantage, taking into account different group configurations that can support children's learning. And finally, in Chapter 6, we address a question that is probably at the top of every administrator's and teacher's list: How do we know children are learning? We provide strategies for monitoring children's progress so that you can tailor instruction to children's needs.

Throughout the book, we've added a number of features to support our view that content-rich vocabulary instruction is essential for children's achievement. You'll find teacher–child interactions taken directly from our studies that provide vivid accounts of children's capabilities. You will also find additional resources, both here and on the web, of ideas that can be implemented immediately in the classroom. In each chapter we have also added ideas to support home–school connections, recognizing the important role parents play in children's vocabulary development. Finally, in various places throughout the chapters, we have included issues to think about, hoping that these questions will encourage the professional community to consider additional activities to support high-quality vocabulary instruction.

The Common Core State Standards reform provides us with a unique opportunity to engage children in meaningful instruction about words. This book is designed to help you take advantage of it.

Why Words Are Important

It seems almost intuitive that developing a large and rich vocabulary is central to learning to read. Logically, children must know the words that make up written texts in order to understand them, especially as the vocabulary demands of content-related materials increase in the upper grades. Numerous studies (e.g., Beck & McKeown, 2007; Stanovich & Cunningham, 1992) have documented that the size of a person's vocabulary is strongly related to how well that person understands what he or she reads, not only in the primary grades, but in high school as well.

Yet here's the practical problem. Right from the beginning of schooling, there are profound differences in vocabulary knowledge among young learners from different socioeconomic groups. Just consider the following statistics: By age 3, a child's interaction with his or her family has already produced significant vocabulary differences across socioeconomic lines, differences so dramatic that they represent a "30-million word catastrophe," according to Betty Hart and Todd Risley (2003). Recent analyses (Rodriquez & Tamis-LeMonda, 2011) indicate that environmental factors associated with vocabulary development and emergent literacy skills are already present among children as early as 15 months of age. By 1st grade, unfortunately, the repercussions become all too clear (Graves, 2006): children from higher-SES groups are likely to know about twice as many words as lower-SES children, putting these children at a significantly higher risk for school failure.

Even more disturbing, however, is that these statistics are often treated as inevitable, more or less a by-product of poverty or low-income status. Think of the consequences! This would mean that these children could be designated as reading failures before they ever enter through the schoolhouse doors.

Luckily, there is now a rich and accumulated new knowledge base that suggests a far different scenario. Consider these statistics:

- The highest rate of vocabulary development occurs during the preschool years; therefore, it represents a crucial time when we can intervene (Farkas & Beron, 2004).
- Effective vocabulary intervention can ameliorate reading difficulties later on. Children with resolved vocabulary delays can go on to achieve grade-level expectations in 4th grade and beyond (Bishop & Adams, 1990).
- The quantity, quality, and responsiveness of teacher and parent talk can effectively *mediate* socioeconomic status, thereby ensuring children's growth in receptive and expressive vocabulary (Mol & Neuman, 2012).
- Gains in oral vocabulary development can predict growth in comprehension and later reading performance (Elleman, Lindo, Morphy, & Compton, 2009).

This means that, in contrast to dire prognostications, there is much we can do to enable children to read and read well. Although we certainly have more to learn, the good news is that we now have an accumulated body of evidence on the characteristics of effective vocabulary instruction. And it turns out that this news couldn't come at a better time.

THE AGE OF COMMON CORE STATE STANDARDS

You might say that we are entering into a new age of educational reform: the Age of Common Core State Standards. In the distant past, education was a local issue; districts acted on their own to adopt instructional guidelines and curriculum. In recent years, however, education has increasingly become more of a state and even a federal concern. The No Child Left Behind Act, the Bush administration's reauthorization of the Elementary and Secondary Education Act, placed a greater role on the states to enact standards, assessments, and accountability. In 2010, state governments took their turn, becoming more proactive in educational reform. The Council of Chief State School Officers and the National Governors Association, working with the organization Achieve, set out to create world-class standards that would essentially create a shared vision of what all students should know and be able to do in all grades, kindergarten through high school.

The reason that this is relevant for those in early education on up is that 46 states and the District of Columbia have adopted these Common Core Standards in English Language Arts and Mathematics. The Standards don't define *how* teachers should teach, but they do tell them *what* to teach. Further, starting in 2014–2015, state tests will be geared toward measuring whether or not students are achieving these Standards. In essence, education is moving toward a more unitary system with a shared vision of expectations for student learning. (All Common Core documents are available at www.corestandards.org.)

These Common Core Standards represent a sea change in how we think about early literacy and reading, in particular, even before children enter kindergarten and throughout the early grades. Here, in a nutshell, are some of the design features:

- **A cumulative model of expectations:** It used to be called "spiraling," but the principle is the same. From grade to grade, similar Standards will increase in complexity. For example, in kindergarten, children will be expected to "ask and answer questions about key details in a text, with prompting and support." In grade 1, you'll see the same exact Standard, although the children will now be required to do it on their own.
- **Informational texts:** Right from the start, the Standards place greater emphasis on listening to and eventually reading informational books. In this respect, the Standards focus on the integration of knowledge and ideas through text. Further, there is the expectation that children will be able to cross traditional genre boundaries and compare and contrast text features; for example, children might listen to an informational book about insects one day and a story about insects the next day, and then be asked about the connections between the two. Children will be expected to learn about key subject areas, particularly science and history, through texts.

  Certainly, this does not mean that we are going to abandon the children's literature or stories that we all have come to know and love. Rather, it simply means a greater balance between literary storybooks and informational texts.

- **Challenging materials:** There is greater emphasis on stretching students to meet the demands of reading harder text than before. In the past, we used to try to meet children's needs by selecting reading materials according to their instructional level; in some cases, when they have difficulty comprehending text, we'll even choose a lower-readability text and have them gradually build up speed for more challenging materials. The Common Core Standards use a very different model. Here, children are required to read grade-level text. Your job as teacher will be to help them learn through these more challenging texts without telling children what the texts say. For example, you might focus on the organizational features of the text, the headings and subheadings in text, or the use of the glossary to unlock the meaning of words in context.
- **An integrated model of literacy:** Although the standards are divided into reading, writing, speaking and listening, and language, there is an expectation that all of these skills work together. You'll see that even young kindergartners are expected to engage in rich conversations that place a greater emphasis on their abilities to build arguments from evidence in the text, whether it is read to them or they read it themselves.
- **An integrated media environment:** There is a greater recognition that today's "texts" don't come only through one medium—print. As all of us know, a high volume of information comes through print and nonprint media forms, both old and new. The Common Core Standards encourage teachers to make use of multimedia, as it's embedded into every aspect of today's curriculum. Children will need to be able to gather, comprehend, evaluate, and synthesize information and ideas through different forms of media.

In short, these Standards focus on results rather than on means. They establish clear goals and expectations that are designed to help children succeed in a world in which the development of information capital is increasingly important. And whether they are ultimately successful in achieving these lofty goals depends on us—teachers—and how well we implement these new Standards in the classroom.

ALL ABOUT WORDS

How do these Common Core Standards relate to oral vocabulary development? And, for those who work with preschoolers or even younger children, how do K–12 standards affect what we teach? Here's why you need to be informed about these Standards: It is impossible for children to read and understand what they read without a strong foundation in oral vocabulary development. Without vocabulary knowledge, words are just words—without much meaning. If we are to help children take on seriously challenging texts, then we need to give them word and world knowledge to bring to these texts. Given that most oral vocabulary development grows from a massive immersion in the world of language, there is not a moment to wait.

The purpose of this book is to explain our rationale for content-rich oral vocabulary instruction in the age of Common Core Standards in English Language Arts, and to provide you with examples of what it looks like early on, before children enter formal schooling, and in the early primary grades. We first start by describing some of the common myths about oral vocabulary development, which have often led to a lack of attention for this important topic in school instruction. We then move to a set of instructional principles that should guide your work. Throughout the book, we highlight research-based practices that have come from our own research studies, as well as syntheses of research conducted with over 7,000 children (Marulis & Neuman, 2010, in press). Together, these findings make it abundantly clear: High-quality, developmentally appropriate instruction in oral vocabulary instruction can make an enormous difference in children's lives, both in the short term and in the long term, helping all on the road to becoming good readers and writers.

COMMON MYTHS ABOUT ORAL VOCABULARY DEVELOPMENT

Before proceeding to the key principles of oral vocabulary instruction, first let's take a look at some of the common myths about vocabulary. Like many myths before them, these notions may contain some partial truths, almost like folk wisdom. For example, some authorities once claimed that learning was based on the "neural ripening" of the brain; applied to reading, this reflected a philosophy of "wait and see" until the child appeared "ready" for instruction. Research and writings in the 1950s and 1960s by cognitive psychologists such as Bruner (Bruner, Olver, & Greenfield, 1966) provided powerful evidence that early childhood was crucial in the cognitive development of an individual. This conclusion led to designing new opportunities to engage children in early learning.

Similarly, a number of myths have been perpetuated about oral vocabulary development, which in many ways have stymied efforts to promote quality teaching early on. Recent evidence has called into question these notions. This new research suggests that we can not only improve children's vocabulary—we can *accelerate* it with instruction. These new findings have powerful implications for further reading development and content learning.

The following myths are at the top of our list.

Myth 1: Children Are Word Sponges

Children seem to pick up words prodigiously and quite effortlessly. It looks natural. In their classic study, for example, Carey and Bartlett (1978) taught preschoolers a new color word simply by requesting, "You see those trays over there? Bring me the *chromium* tray. Not the red one, the *chromium* one." When their memory for the new word was assessed 1 week later, the majority of children (63%) were able to correctly identify which color was chromium. Since this experiment, the term *fast mapping*—the notion that words can be learned based on a single exposure—has become common parlance to explain the extraordinary rate at which children seem to pick up words early on.

Today, however, there is ample evidence to suggest that children do not learn words through "fast mapping" (Bloom, 2000). Rather, they learn words by predicting relationships between objects and sounds, which become more accurate over time. Word learning is incremental (Nagy, Anderson, & Herman, 1987). Evidence for this comes from children's struggles to understand color words. Although infants can distinguish between basic color categories, it is not until about age 4 that they can accurately apply these individual color terms (Rice, 1980). Typically, words such as *red* or *yellow* may appear in their vocabulary; however, their application of these words to their referents may be haphazard and interchangeable.

Children, then, may have knowledge of these words, but this knowledge will be far from complete. Rather, word learning in most cases requires many exposures over an extended period of time (Biemiller & Boote, 2006). With each additional exposure, the word may become incrementally closer to being fully learned.

Myth 2: There Is a Vocabulary Explosion

It is often said that word learning starts rather slowly, then at about 16 months or when a child learns about 50 words, all of a sudden things begin to happen (Gopnik, Meltzoff, & Kuhl, 1999). Word learning begins in earnest. Variously called the "vocabulary explosion" or "word spurt," it reflects the apparent dramatic ability of young children to acquire new words—on the scale of learning ten or more new objects and names within a 2- or 3-week period. This notion of a vocabulary explosion may suggest that the optimal time for oral vocabulary development is in these toddler years.

Recent evidence (McMurray, 2007), however, suggests that the "spurt" in word learning does not correspond to any change in rate of word learning, but in the acquisition of vocabulary that students actually integrate into their speech and writing. In other words, it suggests that the vocabulary explosion is a by-product of the variation in the time to learn words. Although children are accumulating words at a constant rate, the written and verbal use of the words accelerates. We see, for example, a similar pattern with receptive and expressive language, with children demonstrating far greater capacity to understand meaning before they are able to effectively express ideas in words.

The course of word learning, therefore, has little to do with vocabulary explosions, bursts, or spurts. In contrast, word learning is cumulative (Nagy & Scott, 2000). The high-performing student who knows many thousands of words has learned them not by having received a jolt of oral language early on, but by accruing bits of word knowledge for each of the thousands of words encountered every day. By the end of high school, one estimate is that college-ready students will need to acquire about 80,000 words (Hirsch, 2003). This means that we should immerse students for extended periods in oral and written vocabulary experiences throughout their instructional years.

Myth 3: Storybook Reading Is Sufficient for Oral Vocabulary Development

Reading books aloud to children is a powerful and motivating source for vocabulary development (Bus, Van Ijzendoorn, & Pellegrini, 1995). We now have a large corpus of research showing that children learn words through listening to and interacting with storybooks. Nevertheless, recent studies have begun to question whether incidental instruction through book reading may be substantial enough to significantly boost children's oral vocabulary development (Juel, Biancarosa, Coker, & Deffes, 2003). Several meta-analyses (Mol, Bus, & deJong, 2009; Mol, Bus, deJong, & Smeets, 2008; National Early Literacy Panel, 2008), for example, have reported only small to moderate effects of book reading on vocabulary development. Mol and her colleagues (2008) examined the added benefits of dialogic reading, an interactive reading strategy, on children's vocabulary growth and reported only modest gains for 2- to 3-year-old children. Further, these effects were reduced to negligible levels when children were 4 to 5 years old or when they were at risk for language and literacy impairments.

This means that exposure to words through storybooks is not likely to be potent enough to narrow the substantial gap for children who may be at risk for reading difficulties. Rather, to improve children's oral vocabulary development, teachers will need to augment the read-aloud experience with more intentional strategies that require children to process words at deeper levels of understanding.

Myth 4: We Do It All the Time

Most teachers try to consciously engage children in active experiences that involve lots of conversation throughout the day. In the course of a science activity, a teacher may explain a word to help children understand the context. She might briefly pause during the lesson and say, "That's the *predator*. That means he wants to eat the frog," providing a brief explanation that fits the context of the story. Or during a discussion around morning message, a teacher might use the word *celebrate* and then say, "*Celebrate* means to do something fun" when describing a birthday activity. These events represent important teachable moments—informal opportunities to engage in word learning, somewhat parallel to the types of language exchanges between parents and their children.

The problem is, however, that over the course of the 20,000 hours parents and children have spent together in the home *before* entering school, these words are likely to have been repeated frequently. Teachers do not have that luxury. In our study of 55 kindergarten classrooms (Wright & Neuman 2011), for example, we found that although teachers provided over eight of these word explanations per day, they were rarely if ever repeated more than one time. Further, words selected for teachable moments were different across classroom settings. Far too predictably, our study reported that children who attended schools in the most severely low-income neighborhoods were likely to hear far fewer explanations, with those explanations offered at lower difficulty levels, than children in middle- and upper-income areas.

With the implementation of the Common Core State Standards, children will be expected to understand content-related words in science and history. This means that we cannot rely on teachable moments alone to help children develop word meanings. Rather, we will need to be proactive in selecting words that have greater application to academic texts with increasingly complex concepts.

Myth 5: Just Follow the Vocabulary Scope and Sequence in Our Core Reading Program

Several years ago, my colleagues and I examined the prevalence of oral vocabulary instruction in core reading programs at the preK level (Neuman & Dwyer, 2009). We found a dearth of instructional guidance for teachers, despite some "mentioning" of words. Since then, we turned our attention to kindergarten and 1st-grade materials, focusing on the four most commonly used core curricula, to examine the breadth and depth of oral vocabulary instruction—the pedagogical features of instruction and how these features might align with research-based evidence on vocabulary development.

Despite greater attention to words in elementary curricula, our results indicated tremendous disparity across curricula (Wright & Neuman, in press). For example, one curriculum listed an average of 20 target vocabulary words per week to be taught, whereas another listed, on average, only 2. Further, the criteria for which words were selected to teach remained a mystery. In one curriculum, words were selected based on the weekly stories. In other curricula, we could find no organizing principle for the selection of words at all. Finally, using three different criteria, we found that many of the vocabulary words selected for instruction were far too easy to warrant school-based instruction.

This means that until such materials are developed, teachers are going to have to rely on a set of research-based principles to ensure that all students receive the quality of oral vocabulary instruction they need. In the age of Common Core Standards, students will need a specialized language—some describe it as academic language—to convey their ideas and that facilitates the development of more complex concepts in multiple disciplines. And our efforts to enhance the ability of all children to communicate in academic language and academic thinking through oral vocabulary development must begin early.

KEY PRINCIPLES FOR TEACHING ORAL VOCABULARY DEVELOPMENT

Although there is certainly more to learn, we now have a growing research consensus about the characteristics of effective vocabulary instruction. Using evidence from our two recent meta-analyses synthesizing research from 75 vocabulary studies (Marulis & Neuman, 2010, in press), as well as our own studies examining some of the mechanisms for word learning (Kaefer & Neuman, 2011), five principles emerge to enhance oral vocabulary development, as described next.

Key Principle 1: Children Need Both Explicit and Implicit Instruction

Children benefit from explicit instruction. That is, children who are given teacher-friendly definitions of words or other attributes of the words to be learned are more likely to remember them. Prior to the beginning of a story, for example, a teacher might begin by introducing several words that are integral to the story. For example, the teacher might use a strategy developed by Coyne, McCoach, and Kapp (2007) to encourage children to listen for each of the "magic words" during the story reading, and to raise their hands whenever they hear one. A teacher might say to students, "Oh good. Some of you raised your hands! What word did you hear? Yes, the word *peculiar.* When Anansi said the word *seven,* a peculiar thing happened. *Peculiar* means strange or different."

Our syntheses of research reported that vocabulary gains were significantly higher when words were identified explicitly rather than implicitly (e.g., learning words by listening to a story). However, here's something to keep in mind: The largest gains were made when teachers provided *both* explicit and implicit instruction. Silverman (2007), for example, found that engaging children in acting out words after explicitly defining them enhanced word learning as measured by standardized assessments later on. In other words, when teachers made children aware of the meaning of the words and then engaged them in using those words in a meaningful context, children achieved greater gains than from explicit instruction alone.

Key Principle 2: Be Intentional in Word Selection

Given that there are only so many words we can teach—for example, one estimate is a total of about 400 words in a year, we must carefully select the words that we plan to teach. Beck and McKeown (2007) have argued that words for vocabulary instruction should be selected from the portion of word stock that comprises high-utility sophisticated words (Tier 2) that are characteristic of written language. For example, instead of using the words *keep going,* a Tier 2 word might be *maintain;* instead of the word *lucky* one might use the word *fortunate.* These words are domain general, and are likely to relate to more refined labels for concepts that may enhance children's verbal functioning. Studies of "Text Talk," a strategy used by Beck and her colleagues (Beck, McKeown, & Kucan, 2002) to engage children in rich language instruction, have shown impressive results with kindergarten and 1st-grade children, demonstrating vocabulary gains about twice as large as those resulting from read-aloud studies. Given this research-based evidence, the Common Core Standards have adopted this heuristic for selecting words to teach.

However, our research suggests that it's also important to consider content-related words very early on. These are words that will be critical for developing knowledge in key subject areas. For example, vocabulary related to living things, such as *habitat, organism,* and *protection,* can help children talk about and learn about key science-related concepts; moreover, science vocabulary words such as *compare, contrast, observe,* and *predict* are fundamental inquiry words used not only in science but in all subject areas. In our research, we found Head Start preschoolers highly capable of learning and retaining these and similar words over time. Introducing students to content-related vocabulary, therefore, helps them to build word knowledge and concepts essential for developing knowledge systematically from texts.

Key Principle 3: Build Word Meaning Through Knowledge Networks

You might say that words represent the tip of the iceberg; underlying them is a set of emerging interconnections and concepts that these words represent. According to Stahl and Nagy (2006), it is the rich network of concepts and facts accompanying these words that drives children's comprehension. Thus, helping children to learn about words in clusters that represent knowledge networks has been shown to strongly support children's inferential reasoning and comprehension. For example, if you know the word *oar,* you probably also know something about rowboats and paddling. Teaching words in categories such as "healthy foods" (e.g., *fruit, vegetable, protein*) also aids in the retention of these words.

Recent evidence for the support of teaching words in knowledge networks comes from two large-scale studies of vocabulary interventions for low-income preschoolers. Pollard-Durodola and her colleagues (2011), for example, used a number of useful strategies to help children share semantic similarities between words. Strategies such as encouraging children to look at two pictures cards and make inferences about how these words work together helped them make comparisons of concepts. In our World of Words (WOW) curriculum (Neuman, Dwyer, Koh, & Wright, 2007), we teach words related to a semantic category. For example, children learn words associated with "parts of the body," such as *abdomen, lungs, heart,* and *brain,* while focusing on the common features of the category (e.g., "parts of the body" means these are attached to the body). We then engage children in playful activities called "time for a challenge" and ask them questions such as, "Are eyeglasses part of the body?" or "Is hair part of the body?" (Some children argue that hair is not part of the body because their daddies are bald!)

We found that clustering words within categories facilitated children's comprehension and provided promising evidence of accelerating word learning. For example, we showed a picture of a word not taught—in this case, *ankle*, and asked them, "Is an ankle a part of the body?" Children who received instruction reported, "Yes, because it helps you walk," whereas a comparison child not receiving instruction just said, "Yes, 'cause." Similarly, children who received our vocabulary curriculum were able to apply their categorical information to new words, suggesting that they were using the semantic information about categories to make inferences and generalizations.

Finally, helping children understand how words build knowledge networks facilitates our ability to make teaching them more meaningful. This represents a far cry from our analysis of vocabulary in core curricula in which a teacher might be guided to teach the words *platypus* and *around* on the same day (Wright & Neuman, in press). Rather, children learn best when words are presented in integrated contexts that make sense to them. A set of words connected to a category such as "energy" can help children not only remember the words themselves but the linkages in meaning between them.

Key Principle 4: Children Need Repeated Exposure to Gain Vocabulary

Children are most likely to learn the words they hear the most. Findings from a large number of correlational studies on language have shown that frequency of exposure strongly predicts word learning, and seems to have long-range consequences for later language and reading levels (Harris, Golinkoff, & Hirsh-Pasek, 2011). Although this finding is often mentioned in the literature, what is new is that we may have underestimated the amount of frequency required to learn words. For example, in attempting to better understand how many repetitions might be needed to learn a novel word, Pinkham, Neuman, and Lillard (2011) involved 60 4-years-olds in a word-learning task. First, they identified the pseudo-word (e.g., *toma*) for the child, and then they engaged in playing a game of toss with the *toma*, followed by a brief assessment of the word. Twelve children heard the new word repeated 3 times; another 12 children heard the word repeated 6 times; and so forth, for 9, 18, and 24 repetitions. Only 20% of the children who heard the word three times remembered it; in fact, it wasn't until after *24 repetitions* that the majority of children (80%) successfully remembered the word.

The point, of course, is not that all words need 24 repetitions. How-ever, this research does suggest that children need many more encoun-ters with new words than we may have previously suspected. Strategies such as repeated reading have been shown to be effective in helping chil-dren acquire new words. In addition to repeated readings, children may also benefit from rich explanation of newly encountered words. Rich explanations often include as much information as possible about the new word, including information conveyed through defining, providing synonyms, pointing to illustrations, and using the words in other con-texts. These explanations can also give teachers further opportunities to repeat new words, thereby providing children with additional exposures. Another way to build repetition actually goes back to our previous point of teaching knowledge networks. Categories and semantic clusters pro-vide a built-in mechanism for repeating words in meaningful contexts.

At the same time, it is also important for teachers to expose chil-dren to additional contexts in which the word might be used. Silverman and Hines (2009), in their work with second language learners, sug-gest that multimedia can be highly effective for enhancing the mean-ings of words. Their research showed that the gap between non-ELL and ELL children in knowledge of targeted words significantly nar-rowed. They found that video could help children learn by represent-ing words in more than one media format, clarifying the instructional dialogue and adding more information to make sense of words that they are learning. Our research, as well, has shown that the addition of dynamic visuals and sounds in video accompanied by informa-tional books provides children with multiple strategies for acquiring word knowledge. Together, this research highlights that frequency of exposure in a variety of meaningful contexts over an extended period of time enhances word learning. Further, children may continue to benefit from additional exposures to a word and its meaning even if they appear to already understand the word.

Key Principle 5: Ongoing Professional Development Is Essential for Teachers to Accelerate Children's Oral Vocabulary Knowledge

The results of our meta-analyses suggest that children's oral vocab-ulary development is highly malleable, and can be significantly im-proved through intervention. However, these analyses also showed that untrained teachers and teachers with limited educational backgrounds were not as effective in helping children make significant gains in vocabulary. Similar findings have been reported in meta-analyses by Mol and her colleagues (2008). This research highlights the importance of ongoing professional development for teachers and aides who regularly work with children who might need additional instruction.

What types of training may be critical for professional development? Because many of our core programs do not provide sufficient guidance for teachers, as described earlier, in this book we will focus on how teachers might create systematic opportunities for children to learn words and to ensure that they receive a high-quality variety of oral vocabulary instruction. We'll describe rich and varied vocabulary experiences as well as strategies to enrich your verbal environment in the classroom through engaging discussions and collaborations among students. We'll also emphasize helping children to become word "conscious," aware of the world of words around them. Children who are conscious of words regularly enjoy using them in different settings, and are eager to learn new ones (Graves, 2006; Scott & Nagy, 2004). In our projects, we find that preschoolers become fascinated with learning sophisticated words such as *camouflage* when talking about insects or *echo-location* in their conversations about marine mammals, repeating these words in their play to the delight of those around them.

Very recently, we have drawn from our work with young children the notion of an instructional regime as part of teacher's ongoing work in the classroom. This pattern of instruction involves several key steps:

- identifying words that need to be taught,
- defining these words in a child-friendly way,
- contextualizing words into varied and meaningful formats,
- reviewing words to ensure sustainability over time, and
- monitoring children's progress and reteaching if necessary.

This instructional regime, applied at any grade level, promotes greater attention to the depth of processing words and their meanings, and can provide a critical roadmap for the future planning of instruction.

Taken collectively, these five principles of oral vocabulary development, in effect, highlight an approach that is designed to help children unlock the complexities of texts that we see throughout the Common Core State Standards. Given that these Standards will place greater emphasis on students' abilities to build arguments from evidence in texts, these instructional principles will give them the armature to engage in academically enriching conversations that can be fulfilling and highly rewarding.

Common myths are often based on some partial truths that have since been debunked or at least shown to have serious flaws in their logic. This is the case with oral vocabulary development. In the past, we have often described young children as "word wizards," "word sponges," "lexical vacuum cleaners"—all denoting the supposedly easy process of vocabulary development. Too often, it has been assumed that word learning is natural and that the conditions in classrooms provide spontaneous opportunities for vocabulary development.

Teachable moments are important; however, they will not be sufficient for students to engage in complex texts. Rather, we will have to be much more strategic about word learning than our previous standards or instructional guidelines have acknowledged. Recent evidence indicates that children need planned, sequenced, and systematic vocabulary instruction. This means selecting words, concepts, and ideas that matter most to children right from the very beginning of schooling. Many children from high-poverty circumstances will have had fewer experiences with the academic language that the Standards require. Children who enter school in these situations will need skillfully developed instruction that not only improves their word knowledge and concepts, but actually accelerates its development, maximizing the limited time they have in school.

Oral vocabulary development is foundational for learning to read. It is the entry point to concepts and comprehension. We cannot leave it to chance. Consequently, our goal in this book is to support teachers in their development of vocabulary instruction. We hope to engage our readers in tapping children's enormous potential, by providing opportunities for teachers to discuss, describe, and develop the word knowledge and world knowledge that children will need for grappling with the complexities of text. Children's future success in reading depends on it.

THINK ABOUT IT

It's circle time in this kindergarten class, and the teacher is reading a favorite storybook, *Rainbow Fish and the Whale*. As she reads, she stops and points to the picture of the whale. "Look," she says to the children, "Here's a whale and its baby. A baby whale is called a *calf*," as she continues on to the next page. The word is never repeated.

- Which "myths" about oral vocabulary instruction might this teacher hold?
- What "principles" of vocabulary instruction could she use to enhance this instruction?

Some Reflections

This teacher used a "teachable moment" to introduce children to an interesting new word. We know that providing a child-friendly definition of a word in a meaningful context is helpful for developing vocabulary knowledge.

At the same time, it's useful to remember that children are not "word sponges" (Myth 1). Further, brief explanations of words during teachable moments will not be sufficient for building deep and lasting understandings of word meanings (Myth 4).

Here's what would be helpful to consider *in addition* to the teachable moment. In this case, the teacher might return to this *content* word outside of the story. She might ask children to think about other baby animals that are called *calves*. She could talk about alternate explanations of the word *calf* (e.g., "Simon says, 'touch your calf'") and have children consider the multiple meanings of words in different contexts. Further, she might make a chart or read additional books about other words for adult and baby animals (e.g., pup, cub, chick) to help children deepen their networks of knowledge and vocabulary words. In each case, she may provide more explicit and frequent examples to build children's knowledge of the meaning of words.

2 Creating a Vocabulary-Rich Environment

For us, words may be intriguing and fascinating in their own right; for children, however, it is in the pursuit of learning about their worlds and developing special expertise that makes word learning so meaningful. Learning "all about words," especially for young children, therefore must be highly connected with activities children view as interesting and important. This is why early childhood programs that provide children with a rich array of science investigations—activities that support mathematical reasoning and problem-solving skills—are optimal for vocabulary learning. You can't talk and use rich vocabulary words if you have nothing to talk about.

In the age of the Common Core State Standards, children will be expected to know a lot of words, and their multiple meanings. The Standards build on the notion of learning as a developmental progression, designed to help children develop and revise their knowledge and abilities throughout their schooling. What children are capable of learning, therefore, is not simply a function of age or grade level or what is "developmentally appropriate." Rather, learning is contingent on the rich educational experiences children may have and their opportunities to learn. We now know, for example, that children can use lots of words in many interesting contexts and can reason conceptually much earlier than was previously believed.

The environment can help set the stage for these rich vocabulary experiences. It doesn't do the teaching for us, but it can be a powerful support. In this chapter, we will focus on the physical and verbal environments, and how they may enhance the kinds of conversations about and connections between words and their uses. Because the allure of language is in its use, vocabulary experiences are intimately connected to the settings in which they occur.

ORGANIZING YOUR VOCABULARY-RICH ENVIRONMENT

The environment should be rich with opportunities to use language. Rather than littering your environment with print, consider infusing it with words—interesting, content-rich words. For example, in our World of Words curriculum, we teach children about insects and how camouflage helps to protect these small creatures from predators. For weeks on end, we found that the word *camouflage* (which is a fun word to say) would often pop up in the children's independent activities and investigations. Children even attempted to camouflage themselves, dressing up in ways to blend into their environment.

Think about your classroom as an ideal conversation space for giving children time and practice to play with words that you may have introduced through more planned instruction. The more you use your environment as an extension of your teaching (not as a replacement for it), the better children will use the environment and learn from it. Learning doesn't work by osmosis, with children merely absorbing knowledge from the environment; rather a quality environment

allows for child choice and loads of practice, and encourages children to make words their own.

THE PHYSICAL ENVIRONMENT

Let's first consider the physical environment. In our classrooms, we begin by carving out spaces, almost as if they were small areas in a home, with nooks or low partitions. These smaller spaces encourage social interaction and conversation, and tend to reduce overall noise levels. Smaller spaces also afford children the independence and "think time" that they need to engage in purposeful activity. You might consider using bookshelves and other types of shelving to create these pockets of activity.

We use print very strategically. Environments should be well defined, but they should not become a labeling nightmare. Simply putting a label next to an object doesn't necessarily help children learn new words. Rather, it is the use of words and understanding of their functions that help children learn them. For example, we created a "Discovery Center" for exploring interesting new discoveries about plants and photosynthesis. Through their activities in this area, children come to learn what scientific inquiry words such as *problem, hypotheses, classify, compare,* and *contrast* are all about. Once children have a conceptual understanding of these words, then knowledge of the printed words comes easily.

In our classrooms, the alphabet is prominently displayed in a way that is accessible to the children (not up by the ceiling). It's also in *one* place—that children can refer to—instead of in many different places. Too often in recent years, we've seen classrooms turned into alphabet environments. Children have difficulty focusing on important activity when there are too many stimuli in the environment. Rather, consider Montessori's notion of the prepared environment, one that supports children's innate desire for order and control of their world.

Good environments support routines that respect children's purposeful engagement. In our settings, materials are clearly organized in conceptually related groups, and are appealing and accessible to children. Deliberately aggregating materials into a network of related materials or objects creates meaningful opportunities for children to have discussions about them.

IN THE CLASSROOM: A VISIT TO THE SCIENCE AREA

When Jack and Marcus arrive at school on Monday, they notice that there are new materials in the science area, so they run over to explore. A large bin is filled with plastic creatures—insects, which the class has been studying, as well as other bugs and small creatures.

Marcus: (grabbing a handful of plastic creatures) There's a lot of *insects* in there!

Jack: Yeah. A lot, but only some *insects*. Not all of them. See. (finds a caterpillar)

Ms. Lisa: I notice that you've found some new science materials. Do you think you can work together to *compare* them and sort them into *categories*?

Marcus: Yeah. I'm gonna find all the insects and you find the other animals. Okay, Jack?

Ms. Lisa: Do you have a plan for how you'll figure out if a creature is or is not an insect?

Jack: Counting the legs is one thing.

Marcus: And the three body *segments*!

Ms. Lisa: This sounds like an excellent plan. I can't wait to see which pile is larger! Do you have a *prediction*?

Marcus: My insect pile is gonna be bigger for sure.

Ms. Lisa: When you're finished sorting, let me know and we can work on counting them together so we know which pile has more creatures in it.

For example, a science area might contain small magnifying glasses, "samples" to magnify, and pencils and paper or notebooks for use in recording their observations. In addition, displays are related to the current classroom themes and investigations, with children-generated, original work. All of these materials make plain that this is the *children's* classroom, reflecting their work and their unique contributions, and not the teacher's. Further, it sends the important message that the classroom environment is a dynamic one, coordinated with ongoing themes that are related to the big ideas being studied in the classroom.

The Classroom Library

Integral to the environment is the classroom library. Think of it not only as a place to display books, but as a place that is used throughout the day for instruction, enjoyment, and information. Children learn a lot through first-hand experiences, but they will need great second-hand experiences in the form of good books to learn about things they might never have the opportunity to directly experience. In our classroom library, we include:

- Covers of favorite books prominently displayed to entice our young children to read (e.g., you can get them free from the library).

- Books (in good condition) that are visually organized in a way that is easily accessible. Sometimes paperback books, with their narrow spines, don't stack well on bookcases. In this case, you might consider open-face bookshelves.

- Books specially tied to the themes that are currently being studied. If you are studying insects, for example, you will want to include books that are useful to the topic and make them available during independent work time. In our libraries, we include information books, storybooks, and what we call "genre benders." These books might be predictable, narrative-like books, but are topic-rich selections in their treatment of the subject. For example, *Have You Seen Bugs?* (Oppenheim, 1996) is a vocabulary-rich book about insects told in rhyme and rhythm that is highly memorable to children.

- A good number of books that include representations of various racial and cultural groups, along with nonstereotypical themes and characters.

- Books that range in text complexity. Include books that are challenging but achievable for children to read. Children will not stretch themselves and learn new vocabulary words with books that include only very simple, colloquial language. Neither, however, will they learn new words if none are accessible to them.

- A book check-out system. It might be ideal to own books, but a library represents a continuous source of wonderful reading experiences with all different types of books. Very early on, we want to promote the library habit. We include a simple strategy for checking books out, even when children are using them within the library. We create a chart using library pockets with an envelope filled with children's names. When children select a book, they place a card with their name in the pocket. It is also a good strategy to get them in the habit of returning books to where they found them after they have enjoyed a good read.

For the library to be especially useful, consider its placement in your room. If it is off in some corner, it sends the message that "reading

is something you do after you finish your work." Rather, think of it more as an integral partner in the work that you do in your classroom. Although we want children to enjoy reading, most of us use books as a source of learning more about a topic.

Finally, we always adhere to the principle of physical proximity. That means that children are likely to use books when they are within reach. Therefore, although a library is an ideal setting for book reading and use, we also always include books in our science areas, theme-based investigations, and special-topic areas. Continually refreshing your collections in libraries and in strategic places throughout your room sends the message that books are integrally related to your on-going classroom activities, standards, and learning goals.

Technology

Increasingly, technology has an important place as a resource tool for vocabulary development and information. Although programs certainly come in all shapes and sizes, and should be carefully evaluated, many computer-related programs provide a rich resource for independent reading and thinking. New e-books, iPads, and smart boards can

TEN GREAT WEBSITES WITH VIDEO CLIPS AND INFORMATION FOR KIDS

- BBC Learning Schools: http://www.bbc.co.uk/schools/
- Exploratorium: The Museum of Science, Art & Human Perception: http://www.exploratorium.edu/
- How Stuff Works: http://www.howstuffworks.com/
- Kids Know It Network: http://www.kidsknowit.com/
- National Geographic Kids: http://kids.nationalgeographic.com/kids/
- National Wildlife Federation Ranger Rick: http://www.nwf.org/Kids/Ranger-Rick.aspx
- Science News for Kids: http://www.sciencenewsforkids.org/
- Switcheroo Zoo Virtual Zoo: http://switchzoo.com/
- Time for Kids: http://www.timeforkids.com/
- U.S. Government's Official Web Portal for Kids: http://kids.usa.gov/

vividly convey materials that children wouldn't otherwise experience. For example, one teacher showed her students a clip from YouTube of astronauts being interviewed from outer space. Fascinated to learn more, within seconds, they found some additional clips on the iPad. It's the immediacy and the quick responses to questions with images as well as words that make technology so compelling to children (and adults).

Some people would even argue that e-books represent a technological advance over traditional book reading, replacing the page with a screen and enlivening the text with rich imagery, sounds, and animation. We wouldn't go quite that far, yet it is clear that children love the "touch and drag," and the ability to manipulate what they want to learn more about with these tools. Because such tools are an important resource for vocabulary and knowledge building, many teachers have begun to include them in their libraries—thus conveying the notion that they are more than just playthings or social networking devices, but also important resources for learning. At the same time, the portability of these devices means that children literally have information at their fingertips—if, of course, they're taught to use them to their advantage. Remember that young children should never have unsupervised access to the Internet. Rather, when adults strategically select videos, websites, games, and e-books,

THINK ABOUT IT: PHYSICAL ENVIRONMENT

- Which parts of your classroom are set up to promote oral language?
- Where can you make improvements to your space?

Here is a checklist to consider for promoting talk by creating an optimal physical environment in your classroom:

Yes	No	Physical Environment (based on items from the Early Language and Literacy Classroom Observation)
		Have I created spaces for one-on-one, small-group, and large-group conversations?
		Have I created an area set aside for book reading?
		Have I organized books in an orderly and inviting way?
		Have I made a variety of books easily available to children?
		Have I changed materials and displays to support the content that children are learning now?
		Have I made books available that are related to the current theme?
		Have I made books available from a variety of genres (e.g., informational books, storybooks, alphabet books, rhyming books)?
		Have I made books available in all areas of the classroom (e.g., science area, block area, dramatic play area)?
		Have I integrated technological supports for children's learning?
		Is there a place to listen to recorded books or e-books?

What We Think About It:

Studies indicate that interactions in the classroom are impacted by the physical environment. A well-prepared environment ensures that the focus is on learning rather than on other distractions. So, small changes—organizing your library so that children can find and select books, updating books to reflect your current topic of study, creating spaces for conversation—can make a big difference in children's level of engagement in your classroom.

children can learn from exciting media resources. The Think About It: Physical Environment feature provides a checklist for evaluating the quality of the physical environment.

However, it is also important to remember that a well-appointed physical environment alone is not sufficient to support children's oral language development. Rather, it is the interactions and conversations that teachers and children have around the materials in these great spaces that are most highly associated with children's oral language development. So, remember that improving the physical environment is only the first step. The rest of this chapter and book address ways that you can make use of materials and instruction together to support children's oral vocabulary development.

ENRICHING THE VERBAL ENVIRONMENT

In the library area, Billy is reading a book on his own, almost studiously looking at the pictures. His teacher comes by and asks, "What are you reading?" Immediately, the following conversation takes place:

Billy: He's walking on the water? (referring to the picture in the book)
Teacher: Looks like he is.
Billy: Walking on it?
Teacher: Literally walking on it. Water has something called water surface tension.
Billy: Yeah.
Teacher: And he's light enough and he can spread his weight so that he can use that surface tension to stay on the water so he doesn't fall in. We're too big; we'd break through it. So don't you try it!

This exchange is an example of the kind of conversation that supports a rich oral vocabulary environment. Notice how the teacher responds actively to Billy's question and extends his understanding in ways that support *his* interests. You might call this active listening, but it is actually something more. It turns out that adult *contingent responsiveness*—their verbal responsiveness to children's queries and cues—has a strong and sustainable impact on children's verbal skills and abilities (Neuman & Gallagher, 1994). Add in socially engaging behaviors (such as a smile and focused attention), and you have many of the key ingredients of an enriching verbal environment.

Notice that the teacher doesn't *talk down* to the child. Billy might not know much about water surface tension now, but you can probably guess that he'll encounter some analogous experience or read something that will connect these experiences. You'll find that children listen carefully when new words and concepts are described in the context of something that compels them. It won't all be taken in the first time they hear these words, but over time these experiences accumulate so that children not only learn new vocabulary, they learn concepts and background knowledge that will serve them well.

Also notice that the teacher uses the experience to extend Billy's understanding. Billy's questions are simple, probably because he's mulling over ideas that he can't quite express right away. His teacher, however, clearly understands what he's seeking—to learn more about how something could walk on water—and adds clarification and further extension.

In our research, we have found that when teachers *ignore* children's questions and queries time and time again, children get the message. They stop asking questions. This, of course, is not because these children no longer have questions, but because they recognize that there is no responsive adult to answer them.

IN THE CLASSROOM: TALK THROUGHOUT THE DAY

Teachers should always be looking for more ways to support children's oral language development. This means modeling language and teaching new ideas and concepts at all times of the day, *even during breaks and transitions*. For example, when children were getting a drink at the water fountains, we heard one wonderful teacher say:

"Olivia and Tamara, you're both wearing stripes today. You remind me of a herd of zebras at a watering hole."

Later, at snack time, she said, "Don't forget to try those carrots. They are filled with beta-carotene, which is what makes them orange. Beta-carotene is a vitamin that helps your body stay healthy. So make sure you're getting your beta-carotene by eating those nutritious carrots!"

This teacher used every possible moment of the day to support children's learning, and children in this classroom picked up on their teacher's enthusiasm for learning by asking questions, having great discussions, and using great vocabulary throughout the day.

BUILDING HOME–SCHOOL CONNECTIONS: SUPPORTING TALK AT HOME

There is strong evidence that the home language environment is a powerful predictor of children's vocabulary development and school success (Hart & Risley, 1995; Weizman & Snow, 2001). Therefore, teachers should encourage parents to talk with their children and reinforce the words and concepts that are learned at school. Unfortunately, when parents ask, "What did you learn at school today?" they often receive the answer, "I don't know."

One strategy to support parents in reinforcing talk at home is a weekly newsletter that shares information about what has been learned in school, displays photos of the children engaged in learning, and provides specific questions for parents to ask their children about what they have learned in school that week. These questions should direct children to talk about specific ideas that were reinforced or discussed in the classroom. For example, here is a list from Mr. Jimenez's weekly kindergarten newsletter:

- Can you tell me how you can politely ask your teacher for help? (Answer: Walk up to your teacher and say "excuse me" rather than yelling to your teacher from across the room.)
- Can you tell me the months of the year and say them in order?
- Can you tell me how the stories *Panda Bear, Panda Bear* and *Brown Bear, Brown Bear* by Eric Carle are similar and different? (Answer: They are similar because they both include animals and they both include a repeated rhyming pattern in the words. They are different because they include different types of animals—the animals in *Panda Bear, Panda Bear* are endangered species, whereas the animals in *Brown Bear, Brown Bear* are more common.)
- Can you tell me about the tools that you used when painting? (Answer: feathers, forks, pipe cleaners, craft sticks, cardboard)
- Can you tell me about the plants you are growing? What type of seeds did you plant? What do they need to grow? (Answer: We planted tomato seeds, and they need soil, water, and sunlight to grow.)

We like to think that every teacher–child exchange has the potential to be an instructional conversation. Think about your words as conveying bits of knowledge, adding to the child's increasingly rich knowledge network each time you talk. You'll see how much children pay attention when they feel they are learning from these conversations. Here are some ways to spark these instructional conversations:

Use Challenging Words

Frequently use words that are not common in day-to-day speech. For example, when talking about the weather, try using less common words in your dialogue, such as "the *meteorologist* said today would be sunny and warm," or let's make *predictions* about the weather." Children love to mimic adult talk, and pretty soon you'll find that the "weather person" in your class is now referred to as the "meteorologist." The other reason we like to use challenging words is that they are natural attention-getters. For example, instead of saying there's too much *noise* in the class, you might say there are too many *disruptions*, or that you are finding these *disruptions disturbing* or even *horrendous*. These words help children to distinguish new and more challenging words from those used in day-to-day talk.

Extend and Clarify

Children's ideas and concepts are evolving as they learn. Often, they have approximations of what a word or a concept might mean that needs further clarification and extension. We want children to try out these approximations with us, as these are a mirror of what they currently know. For example, when learning about insects, we found it is not uncommon for children to think that bees get honey from flowers, instead of nectar from flowers that the bees then convert into honey. As teachers, we can help clarify such misconceptions, but to do so, children must feel free and encouraged to provide their approximations.

Use Abstract Language

When we say to children, "Remember the time we . . ." (fill in the blank), we are using representational language. That is, we are talking about things not immediately present. This type of language, sometimes described as *decontextualized talk*, is enormously helpful in supporting children's ability to engage in abstract thinking—in thinking about words and concepts in more generalized ways than in the here and now. Studies have shown that there are many easy ways to help

ABSTRACT LANGUAGE

Abstract language is language focused on concepts, rather than on concrete items in the everyday environment. For example, if you say "Here's some yogurt" when you give a child a morning snack, this is not abstract language. You have labeled an object in the immediate environment. If you say, "Today's snack is yogurt, which belongs in the dairy food group. Can anyone explain to me why yogurt is considered a dairy product?" then you have moved from the concrete (i.e., yogurt) toward the conceptual (i.e., groups of foods that form a category based on how they are created and produced). Here are some ways to incorporate more abstract language into your classroom:

- Teach children about categories. For example, rather than just saying "This is a daisy," say, "This is a daisy, a type of flowering plant."
- Teach children about relationships. For example, think about relationships such as parts and whole (e.g., a root is a part of a whole plant) and form and function (e.g., the root absorbs water from the ground).
- Teach children about processes (e.g., ask, "What do living things need to survive?").

children shift from the concrete situation to a more abstract conception that implies the use of representational language. For example, when we ask children to put things into categories—common sorting activities—they are engaging in making inferences from the observable to the nonobservable. We might show children pictures of apples, peaches, and bananas and ask, "Can you *compare* these? How are these objects similar or alike in any way?" Such questioning encourages them to synthesize and make generalizations.

You probably are already using abstract or representational language every day in your talk. Accentuate it and use it as frequently as you can. We've highlighted some of the ways that you can engage in these techniques in the accompanying boxed feature.

Use Eye-to-Eye Instruction

Children intuitively know when you are paying close attention to them. Studies have shown that shared focus—through eye-gazing, pointing, or other verbal or nonverbal indications with children—is

central to learning language and vocabulary. It establishes a clear reference, providing children with information about their environment and helping them to make connections from spoken language to real objects. It also establishes a feeling of warmth between you and the child, giving him or her a clear signal that you understand the intentions behind the talk. When we look distracted, and our eyes gaze in all directions, we send a signal that other things are more important than the individual child's question or query. Obviously in busy classrooms, this may be hard to do, but try to take time for each and every child to have your full attention for even a moment every day.

Use Purposeful Talk

This is something that is often overlooked in early childhood classrooms. Right from the beginning, we need to help children respect other children's questions and comments, as well as our own. To do so, we teach children what we call *purposeful talk*, which requires active listening. When a child is talking to the group, others should look at him or her, with a focus similar to the eye-gaze we would have when listening to another individual. When someone makes a comment, the next child might want to begin by saying, "I agree with Abby's comment and I'd like to add. . ."; older children may even use comments such as, "I'd like to elaborate on Tanya's point," indicating that they must have listened to what the previous person had said.

The best way to start the process of purposeful talk is to introduce some key phrases, such as "I agree with," "I'd like to extend," and "I want to disagree with this point." You'll find that when children begin their comments with these simple phrases, it makes for more lively discussions in the classroom. It will also take you off the stage, allowing children to converse with one another, providing opportunities for more prolonged practice using oral language.

QUESTION, COMMENT, OR COMPLIMENT

One way to encourage children to have conversations with each other is to actively teach *pragmatics*, or how to use language in social situations or conversations. A simple way to begin is to encourage children to respond to one another with a question, a comment, or a compliment. Make sure to explain each of these and the differences among them. For example, if one child says, "I think that a caterpillar is not an insect," you can ask, "Does anyone have a question, comment, or compliment in response to this idea?"

Question: Why do you think a caterpillar is not an insect?
Comment: A caterpillar has too many legs to be an insect.
Compliment: I agree with you. I think you know a lot about insects.

TWO MORE WAYS TO ENRICH THE VERBAL ENVIRONMENT

It's always good to remember that the teacher is a role model for the type of talk we hope to hear from children in the classroom. You can model oral language by verbalizing your thoughts for children. Try the following techniques and encourage children to try them as well, with the goal of creating an environment that values using language to express thoughts and ideas.

(Continued)

Parallel Talk

You can help children to develop their oral language by using parallel talk, describing what the child is experiencing. Try talking about what the child may be hearing, seeing, experiencing, or feeling. For example, "I notice that you are touching the bark on that tree trunk. I wonder if it feels rough or smooth when you touch it?" or "I think you might feel frustrated because you are not the line leader right now." As you narrate for children, you model language about both sensory and more abstract experiences. This exposes children to words beyond those they might experience every day and to the more complex language that will support comprehension.

Think-Aloud

You can also use oral language to make your own thoughts and actions more explicit for children. For example, during a read-aloud, you can share what you are doing and thinking: "Right now, I'm wondering why the narrator keeps talking about a bear when we haven't seen a bear in any pictures so far," or "I really hope the baby bird finds his mother soon. He's probably getting sad, tired, and hungry!"

BUILDING HOME–SCHOOL CONNECTIONS
TOPIC: CENTERED SHOW AND TELL

Show-and-tell activities can be very supportive for children's oral language development because children are expected to engage in extended talk, describing an object and its importance. For children who are outgoing and who have strong oral language skills, this can be a very exciting time of the day. For children who are shy or for those who have weaker oral language skills and vocabulary, show and tell can be very challenging. Two ways to support all children during show and tell are to (1) structure these times around a specific topic that the class is studying so that all children feel confident and knowledgeable, and (2) provide language scaffolds so that children know the type of language to use and have a clear idea of what they are expected to say.

For example, during a study of how plants change over the course of the seasons, one prekindergarten teacher asked each child to bring in a fall leaf for show and tell. Each child was expected to tell four things about his or her leaf, ensuring that each child had an extended opportunity to use oral language: (1) Describe the leaf (i.e., tell about its color and its shape), (2) tell where it was found or picked, (3) tell why you selected this particular leaf, and (4) tell whether you think the leaf came from an *evergreen* or *deciduous* plant and why you think this based on what we've been reading and learning at school.

In the note that went home to families about this activity, family members were asked to help their child to find a leaf and also to help their child practice talking about leaves by responding to the four prompts. By the time children arrived at school, they were excited and prepared to talk to their friends. Here are some of the descriptions children gave:

Jesse: This leaf is dark green and pointy. I picked it from a tree in my grandma's yard. I picked it 'cause I liked how pricky it is. I think it's evergreen 'cause it's still green. And, I picked it off the tree, and those other trees in the yard, their leaves have fallen off.

Angela: My leaf is like orangey and red together. It's got some points. My mommy said it's a maple leaf. I got it from the sidewalk under a tree. I think it's deciduous.

Teacher: Why do you think it's deciduous?

Angela: 'Cause it's not green and 'cause it fell off of the tree.

THINK ABOUT IT: ORAL LANGUAGE ENVIRONMENT

Try selecting one or more of the oral language strategies listed in this chapter and implementing it intentionally over the course of a week in your classroom. You might even consider audio or video recording so that you can listen later to see if you have promoted more or higher-level conversations in your classroom. What are the results?

- Were you able to encourage oral language throughout the day?
- Do children have longer conversations?
- Do more children participate in conversations?

(Continued)

- Do children use new words and phrases that you have modeled for them?
- Do children have more conceptual conversations, beyond talk about concrete items and day-to-day routines?

What we think about it:

Young children, who cannot yet read independently, *need* adults in order to learn new oral language. Unlike older children, who can learn new vocabulary by reading on their own, the only way for young children to be exposed to new words and phrases is if an adult says them or reads them aloud. So, one of your most important roles as a teacher is to model the type of talk that you want children to learn. In addition to modeling language, you will need to scaffold children's language development by planning opportunities for them to practice using new words and ideas in purposeful conversations.

SUMMARY

In this chapter, we have highlighted ways in which the physical and verbal environment may support vocabulary development. Classrooms that include a physical environment that supports talk and an enriching verbal environment create opportunities for children to become increasingly *word conscious* (Nagy & Scott, 2000). In these lively environments, there is a disposition about words that is both cognitive and affective. New words are interesting and fun to learn, and there is a growing satisfaction from using them well and from seeing or hearing them used well by others. Words are used in ways that support children's compelling need to understand their worlds. Words, in short, help them to begin to develop the conceptual understandings that underlie much of what they will seek to learn about.

3 Building Children's Vocabulary

Nothing is more precious than instructional time. You don't have much of it, so you will need to think very intentionally about how to use it. Here, then, is the vocabulary conundrum: If students need to know about 80,000 words in order to be college- or career-ready by the end of high school according to the Common Core State Standards, and, realistically, we can only teach about 300 to 500 words per year, how do we get there? How do we build—even accelerate—children's vocabulary to reach this goal?

In this chapter, we'll describe our approach for teaching content-rich vocabulary in the earliest years through the beginning primary grades. We'll show how building children's vocabulary knowledge early on can lead to a self-teaching mechanism that supports vocabulary growth through reading complex texts later on.

THE PROBLEM

Even if you teach preschool now, we want you to imagine your students some 7 years later, when they are about 12 or so. According to the Common Core State Standards, they will be expected to read informational texts in history/social studies and science independently in grade 6, and with some scaffolding, "stretch" to read even two grade levels beyond their current level. This excerpt from *Space Probe. Astronomy & Space: From the Big Bang to the Big Crunch* is an example of the type of text they'll be given:

> A space probe is an unpiloted spacecraft that leaves Earth's orbit to explore the Moon, planets, asteroids, comets, or other objects in outer space as directed by onboard computers and/or instructions sent from Earth. The purpose of such missions is to make scientific observations, such as taking pictures, measuring atmospheric conditions, and collecting soil samples, and to bring or report the data back to Earth. Numerous

space probes have been launched since the former Soviet Union first fired Luna 1 towards the Moon in 1959. Probes have now visited each of the eight planets in the solar system. (Engelbert, 2009, p. 209)

To read with reasonable comprehension, a student needs to understand 95% of the words in this 100-word passage. Knowing that percentage of words will allow the reader to get the main thrust of what is being written, and therefore to guess correctly what the unfamiliar words probably mean. Knowing fewer than that, perhaps only 90%, will generally put the student at the frustration level. This will place the student at a double disadvantage: he or she will miss the opportunity to learn the content of the text, and the opportunity to learn new words.

But here's something equally important to consider: Most teachers could make a good guess at what words students may stumble on—such as *asteroids, comet, atmospheric conditions,* and *space probes.* However, interestingly, even some easier words, such as *soil samples* and *scientific observations,* might prove challenging to the reader. These words may be easy to read, but hard to understand. In other words, the concepts they refer to are demanding; both terms defy simple definitions.

Notice, also, that they all represent content-related words. They are not necessarily sophisticated, as identified by Beck and McKeown (2007) as the type of words that represent more refined labels for concepts. In addition, we wouldn't necessarily call them academic vocabulary—the 7,923 vocabulary terms that students should know as identified by Robert Marzano (2004). Instead, these are all words that have deep connections to the content students will be exposed to in the subject areas of science, social studies, math, and the arts and music. And it is these words and concepts that need to be taught in the early years of instruction.

A CONTENT-RICH APPROACH TO VOCABULARY INSTRUCTION

You might ask, "How do we know what content-related words are most important? Are there particular words and concepts that children will need to know in order to move successfully into the elementary grades and beyond?" It turns out that there is remarkable consensus among the states and the various standards on topics that should be covered in the beginning grades. For those who work with preschoolers, even the most recent cross-walk of the new Head Start Outcomes Framework with the Common Core State Standards is consistent with these themes. For example, let's take a look at the science standards from several states and the requirements for student learning in kindergarten:

KINDERGARTEN SCIENCE STANDARDS IN FOUR STATES

Topic	Texas	California	Michigan	Indiana
Plants	The student is expected to record parts of plants, including leaves, roots, stems, and flowers.	Students know how to identify major structures of common plants (e.g. stems, roots, leaves).	Compare and contrast familiar organisms on the basis of observable physical characteristics (flowering and nonflowering plants, trees, parts of a seed).	Observe plants and describe how they look (i.e., stems, petals, leaves).

In each of these states, there is an expectation that children will learn about plants in the life sciences. Along with developing some of the big ideas about living things (e.g., how things grow; the importance of water, light, and air), there is the expectation that they will able to use the vocabulary associated with these concepts, as well as general terms within the domain. And what you see here is not an anomaly. Even before we had Common Core State Standards in English Language Arts and Math, there were common expectations for student outcomes in all the key domains— science, social studies/history, as well the arts.

These are the words that are critical for children to learn if they are to understand what they read when they begin to read independently. Further, these are the words we want children to know deeply, with great understanding, so that when they get to 6th grade, words like *soil samples* and *scientific observation* are in long-term memory, and therefore, easily recalled when necessary for comprehending complex text.

To help guide you, we have included a list of content-related words that children should know and understand for preK through grade 2 in Appendix B. You'll see that we have clustered them around common topics in these grade levels. We do this intentionally: Teaching vocabulary words and concepts within topics of interest supports meaningful interactions with words rather than rote learning.

For example, here's a sample list of words pertaining to parts of the human body:

abdomen	chest	eyes	heart	organs
brain	cheeks	ears	lungs	spine
blood	chin	eyebrows	muscles	torso

As important as these content-related words are, however, it's impossible to talk about them without using additional words that may act in a supportive role. For example, when you are talking about the human body with children, you are likely to mention our *senses*, and how we learn through *taste*, *touch*, and *smell*.

In the case of the human body, words that help to support their learning include:

observe	examine	feel
predict	notice	touch
discover	recognize	taste

We call words like these *supportive words*—words that help to support children's ability to talk about the topic. In Appendix A, you'll see that we have listed a number of these important supportive words that will be used across different topics and domains.

In addition, we try to include a number of "challenging words"—words that have a strong conceptual load, and typically connect to our content-related words. For example, the words *nourishment* and *energy* are words that fundamentally relate to the human body and reflect big ideas about the topic. Focusing on these three categories of words—content related, supportive, and challenging—will build both breadth and depth in your vocabulary instruction.

The reason that these distinctions in terms—content-related, supportive, and challenging words—are important is that we teach them differently. In the case of content-related words, we provide many opportunities through our teaching and independent practice for children to deeply engage in understanding the words and the concepts

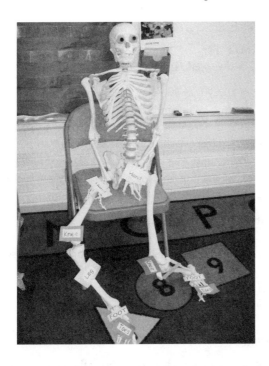

that may underlie them. However, in the case of supportive words, we are more likely to model them in the context of our instruction. For example, a teacher might ask when reading a story to children, "What do you predict will happen?" After a child responds, the teacher might answer, "Yes that's a good prediction—a good educated guess for what might happen next." Supportive words, then, are somewhat easier to teach because teachers will use them frequently in the course of conversation and because they serve a particular function that can be well defined.

On the other hand, we will introduce challenge words as a way of stretching children's understanding, with the expectation that these words will be learned over time. In many respects, as their experiences develop and accumulate, their understandings of these words will progress over time. They are building knowledge networks, and the words often reflect the big ideas that are foundational to them.

You should note two important points in our approach to teaching vocabulary. First, if you look at the full sequence for this topic in Appendix A, you'll see that we expect children to learn far more words than in previous approaches. For example, most vocabulary programs only teach between 6 and 10 words per week, yielding—if

THINK ABOUT IT:
SELECTING VOCABULARY TO TEACH

Choose a topic of study that you plan to address in your classroom. Select key vocabulary that you will plan to teach this year. Remember to: (1) Think about key concepts children should learn and choose words to support these concepts, (2) select words that will help children to become more knowledgeable about these key concepts, and (3) choose topic words that are important for supporting ongoing discussion or read-alouds related to the content you are teaching.

- Were you able to find a topic of study where you could add vocabulary instruction?
- Were you able to tie new vocabulary words to key concepts that you plan to teach?
- Were you able to think of a large set of words to teach using the instructional sequence?

What we think about it:

Planning for vocabulary instruction does not take long, but it is incredibly important to ensuring that the children in your class learn new words. We have found that teachers typically teach word meanings only in teachable moments, when a tricky word comes up in conversation or in a book. Although teachable moments are a great way to enhance the language environment in the classroom, for many children, this type of teaching is just not enough. To retain new vocabulary, children need systematic opportunities to learn word meanings and to practice and review the same words over time. To implement this type of instruction, you will need to have a plan.

Taking time to sit down and think about word selection will help you to feel prepared. Once you know *what* you plan to teach (i.e., which words), then you can focus on building opportunities into your daily routines where children can learn and practice their new vocabulary.

all words are remembered—about 360 words taught throughout a year. Contrary to those approaches, we believe that children will not be able to be successful in reading unless they accumulate a rich storehouse of words and concepts. Combining the content-related, supportive, and challenging words, we teach a total of 50 words for every topic. Second, take a look at the content-related words in

> ## THREE PLACES TO FIND CONTENT VOCABULARY WORDS
>
> 1. **Trade books:** Use both literature and informational books that are related to your topic of study. Look for words that are necessary for describing and discussing your topic.
> 2. **Your curricula:** Think about concepts that children should learn in your curriculum and then consider the vocabulary words they would need to discuss this information.
> 3. **The Internet:** Many teachers address similar topics or use similar curricula in their classrooms. A quick Internet search for your topic and "vocabulary" might help you to find a fantastic list of content words.

particular. You'll notice that some words are familiar (conceptually) for the average kindergarten and 1st-grade student, such as *chin, ears,* and *eyes.* On the other hand, some are quite demanding, such as the words *brain, lungs,* and *torso.* In all of our lists, we try to include words that children will feel competent in using right away, as well as those words that will stretch them to learn. We try to keep the equation of words relatively equal: 50% partially familiar (too familiar would be too easy) and 50% more demanding words to ensure that all students will feel confident that they are capable learners and able to tackle the more difficult words.

A TEACHING SEQUENCE

If you take a look at the typical core reading program in kindergarten or 1st grade, you'll see why vocabulary can be so difficult for some children to learn. Word lists or those words that publishers suggest that you teach often look like this:

platypus	open	around
before	together	move

We suspect that these words were selected because they are in the read-aloud text or the text children will be asked to read. First, notice that the words have no meaningful relationship whatsoever to each other—you'd have to work hard to put together a sentence that uses two or more of these words together. Second, you'll see that some of these words qualify more as supporting words that are best taught within the context of your lesson rather than stand-alone words. For example, it's simply easier to use the words *move* or *around* in context instead of isolating these words for instruction. Finally, given that instructional time is precious, is it worthwhile to spend time teaching the word *platypus* when there are so many other words that need to be taught?

In contrast, our approach focuses on an instructional regime that helps children to build meaningful relationships among words. Our goal is to help them understand words as they relate to concepts. As we teach, we are consciously working to help children organize words and concepts in ways that will enable them to become self-learners. We use a five-step process for teaching our targeted words. As we describe our process, we'll use examples from one of the children's favorite topics—all about marine mammals.

Step 1: Identify Two or Three Exemplar Words Related to Your Topic

Although we will teach many different words, we begin by teaching only a few—those that are especially relevant to our topic. In the case of marine mammals, for example, we first introduce our kindergarten children to the words *dolphin* and *whale.* These are words that children are likely to know something about, and will enable us to build on their natural interests to know more about these fascinating animals. We will use only two terms in the very beginning to allow children to focus on developing a deeper meaning of these words. In this respect, we identify key terms that serve as exemplars for many other related words in our topic. For example, we may begin a topic on "All about Me" by introducing children to words such as *heart* and *brain,* two intriguing parts of our body that can encourage discussion.

On subsequent days, we'll begin to introduce many more words related to the topic. Once children have developed a mental picture of a term, such as for *dolphin,* it becomes much easier to introduce new words such as *manatee* and *sea lion,* along with the characteristics of these wondrous marine mammals, such as the *blubber* they use to keep themselves warm and the *oxygen* they breathe, just like us. Because the words that are selected are meaningful, it becomes easier to slot them into long-term memory. Imagine that someone asked you to remember the words *square, effort,* and *many.* You might be able to recall them immediately, but after some days, you're likely to forget them. Now think about remembering the words *square, triangle,* and *circle*—all types of shapes. You are likely to remember them because they are related to each other. In addition, you'd probably use a generic noun to describe them. For example, you might say, "A square is a type of shape." Although this seems pretty natural to you, the use of generic nouns is related to children's ability to conceptualize, to group common objects together, which allows them to structure their knowledge in ways that are more easily accessible for learning. For example, a noun is generic when it represents a whole class of objects, such as "the *fruit* is juicy and ripe."

Step 2: Provide a Child-Friendly Definition, Description, and Explanation of the New Word

In the past, it was considered good practice to determine what children already know about a word before providing information about it. A common approach was to simply ask children to share aloud what they already know or what they *think* they know about a word. The notion is that you might hear accurate prior knowledge that you can build on or misconceptions that you can correct. However, recent scholars have challenged this view, arguing that misconceptions can be very difficult to correct. Wild guesses or inaccuracies are just as likely to be remembered as a more accurate response. For example, a common misconception concerning the word *dolphin* is that it refers to a type of fish—a dolphin is actually a mammal with certain characteristics that clearly differentiate it from a typical fish.

Even though some children may know a lot about a topic, we always start with a simple explanation, placing all children on common ground. We try to use a succinct description, such as "A dolphin is a marine mammal. That means it lives its whole life in the ocean. It looks like a fish but has lungs and breathes air just like us."

Here's why these simple explanations are powerful. Notice that we are introducing the target word out of the context of a story or read-aloud. Providing an explicit explanation prior to its introduction in context helps children to focus on the word and its meaning. In a sense, it puts the word on center stage. After an explanation, we'll build understanding of the meaning of the word through guided

assistance. There are many ways to do this, but here are some that work especially well:

- They say that "pictures can be worth a thousand words," and this is particularly true for vocabulary development. Use pictures to provide good close-ups of the terms you are trying to convey.
- Play a guessing game. Say, for example, "I'm thinking of a part of the body that helps us breathe," and let children respond to the riddle. You can also encourage them to take turns make their own riddles.
- Try synonyms and antonyms. Children can develop deeper meaning of words by exploring synonyms and antonyms. On one day, you can focus just on synonyms. For example, you can play a game, such as, "Let's see how many words we can think of that mean the same thing as *delicious* in 2 minutes." On another day, play the same game with antonyms, although this is likely to be a bit harder. You'll find that the children will get better and better over time, and will enjoy extending their vocabulary.

ADDITIONAL WAYS TO GIVE INFORMATION ABOUT A NEW WORD

Use Media. Consider using media to give meaning to a word. Brief videos are particularly useful when children may not have the opportunity to experience something in their everyday lives. For example, when we are studying plants, we watch videos about a field of sunflowers or the life cycle of an apple tree. Few early childhood classrooms are likely to have access to these real experiences, particularly for some topics (e.g., marine mammals), so media can serve to build and reinforce understanding of words and concepts. Media also allows children to look at what would normally be slow processes (e.g., a seed growing into a plant) in more exaggerated terms, enhancing the experiences that could only otherwise be simulated in the classroom. For many of the topics that children study in their classrooms, teachers can find brief videos that support children's learning of complex words and concepts. Following these vivid demonstrations, conversations and discussions are bound to be lively.

Make Connections by Teaching Categories. In addition to an explanation or definition, we want children to begin to structure their new knowledge in ways that make it more accessible for learning. We do this by giving information about the word's category: "A fig is a type of fruit," or "An evergreen is a type of plant." We also teach the properties of the category. For example, we teach children that evergreens are similar to other types of plants because they have things in common (e.g., plants are living things; they need sunlight and they need water to grow). In this respect, we help children to build knowledge networks. If you learn a new word, such as *ficus*, and know that it fits into the category of "plant," then you can generalize beyond that simple definition to know that it will need water and sunlight to grow. When you help children understand categories of objects, plants, or animals, you begin to build a more coherent framework for children by making them aware of the relationships among the vocabulary terms being taught. Teaching categories, therefore, is a natural vocabulary builder. It consolidates children's thinking about words, and provides a strategy for understanding new ones.

Relate Words to Key Concepts or "Big Ideas." You can also help children deepen their word knowledge by explicitly linking new vocabulary to the concepts or big ideas that are being taught. For example, in life science

(Continued)

topics we often focus on such "big ideas" as habitat, protection, and life cycle—ideas that cut across different topics and support words that are related to one another at their conceptual level. When we talk about habitat in our work on the human body, we may focus on our home as a habitat. When we talk about marine mammals, they, too, of course have a habitat. These big ideas help to link your curriculum in fundamental ways; children are no longer just moving from one topic to another. Rather, they are building a rich storehouse of words, categories, and concepts along the way.

As we do these kinds of knowledge-building activities, we will continue to increase the number of new words in our work together. We'll soon introduce children to words such as *manatee, walrus,* and *polar bear,* along with the supporting words such *warm-blooded, fin, blubber, oxygen,* and so on. Because these words relate to the concept of marine mammals, children will begin to understand the connections between these words and what they are learning. In other words, by starting out with a firm foundation of understanding with just a few words taught well, we can accelerate children's ability to slot words into meaningful knowledge networks. For example, our studies show that if we introduce the word *manatee*—a sophisticated word for preschoolers and kindergartners—and tell them it's a marine mammal, they will tell us that it's warm-blooded, uses oxygen to breathe, and lives in the ocean.

Step 3: Give Children Many Opportunities for Guided Practice

At this point, children are ready to try out some of these content-rich words with guided practice. This is *not* about sending students off with a worksheet, or letting them engage in an independent activity. Rather, to make sure they're on the right track, we carefully pose questions that gradually lead them from rather easy and familiar examples to more applied examples, using their new words in new contexts. Studies have shown that using new words in multiple contexts can enhance children's depth of processing, and help them make these words their own.

As we mentioned in Chapter 1, we also know that teachers often underestimate the amount of practice children will need. So the challenge here is that we'll need to pick up the pace of guided practice, providing many opportunities for children to respond to questions with sufficient feedback to ensure that they'll be successful.

We use a series of questioning techniques to provide guided practice. As we teach, we use the "hand-over principle," starting with brief, targeted questions and then moving on to those eliciting more open-ended responses. Note that we use open-ended questions only when we're convinced that children will use a specific term or concept correctly in an applied setting. Here is our sequence:

- **Choral recall response.** We'll start by asking questions that encourage a choral response, encouraging all children to respond together. Here's an example:

  Teacher: Is a dolphin a marine mammal?
  Children: Yes
  Teacher: Where does it live?
  Children: Ocean
  Teacher: Do marine mammals breathe oxygen?
  Children: Yes
  Teacher: Then what type of marine mammal breathes oxygen?
  Children: The dolphin

  These questions are fast paced and are designed to grab children's attention and keep them highly engaged. This technique also increases the number of times they're likely to hear the word.

- **Questions that help children apply their new knowledge.** In the next phase, we'll spend time encouraging children to make contrasts and comparisons of terms. In this case, we'll begin to target individual responses so that we get a sense of who might need additional instruction. For example, we'll ask:

  Teacher: How are a whale and dolphin alike? Tanya?
  Child: They are both marine mammals.
  Teacher: Great, and how might they be different? Tameika?
  Child: A whale is fatter than a dolphin.
  Teacher: Yup, that's right, a whale has lots of blubber, and weighs several tons more. How else? Jeremy?
  Child: Dolphins swim in pods, but whales don't.
  Teacher: Great observation!

- **Open-ended responses.** Now we're ready to stretch children's reasoning, creativity, and independence. Open-ended responses are designed to elicit fresh insights and ideas, and are less constrained than recall questions. By the time we move to open-ended responses, we're more confident that children have the background knowledge to build on the new ideas.

  Sometimes we'll use a "think-pair-share" technique to get children to first think about their answers, then share with another student in paired responses, and then share with the whole class any new thoughts or understandings that they've discussed in their pairs. We might begin by asking children a very simple open-ended question, such as "What is your favorite marine mammal, and why?" These types of questions will elicit unique responses that will also interest the other students in the class.

Or you can engage children in picture or word sorts, in which you first provide children with words/pictures that represent two or more categories. For example, you might have pictures of a sea otter, seal, and horse. Ask children to put the pictures in categories, and then give a justification for why they sorted them the way they did. When students provide a rationale, they will undoubtedly use generic nouns, such as "these *animals* are all mammals, but two of them are marine mammals." These are the kinds of generalizations that help to build important concepts.

INTRODUCING NEW WORDS WITH GRADUAL RELEASE OF RESPONSIBILITY

Move from the known to the unknown. One way to engage all children in content-rich vocabulary instruction is to use a familiar prototype or exemplar to bridge children's current knowledge with more complex words and concepts. For example, when we teach about insects, we might use *ant* or *bee* to teach the vocabulary for the basic body parts (i.e., both ants and bees have a head, thorax, and abdomen) and characteristics of an insect. Although most children can name common insects by sight at an early age, they do not necessarily have the conceptual knowledge or vocabulary to link these creatures to the broader category of insects. In fact, most young children would probably say that ants and bees are the same because "they're small" or "they're bugs." Although these are both true statements, this is not the reasoning that would be used by most adults or a biologist.

When we think about content-rich vocabulary instruction, we focus on teaching new words but also on deepening children's understanding of words they already know, and, more important, on helping children to make conceptual connections across words. A child who can explain that both ants and bees are insects *because they have three body parts and six legs* is quickly able to identify a grasshopper as an insect for the same reasons and therefore can use this categorical knowledge to infer information about the grasshopper's likely characteristics, life cycle, and habitat.

Give information before application. The title of this strategy is a silly mnemonic device, but its intent can be the key to ensuring that all children can learn and participate in content-rich vocabulary instruction. In many classroom situations, children are quizzed before they are taught. For example, we've heard teachers begin a discussion of pets by asking questions such as "Can anyone name some pets?" For children who own pets, this is an opportunity to share what they already know, but children who know little about pets are effectively silenced and cannot participate in the classroom conversation. Rather, in our work, we use a *gradual release of responsibility*—a sequence of instruction where we begin by engaging all children in the classroom by teaching words and content knowledge and then later help them to apply their knowledge to challenging discussions and problem-solving experiences.

(Continued)

For example, in the first few days of learning about insects, a teacher would provide a preliminary definition of an insect (i.e., a small creature that has six legs and three body parts); teach words that can identify, describe, and explain an insect (e.g., *abdomen, antennae, thorax*); and give at least one example of a type of insect (e.g., bee, ant). The teacher can use whole-group discussions, picture cards, video clips, and books to present this key information.

It is only after children learn this more basic information that they are asked to use their knowledge to support discussion and application. At this point, "Can anyone name some insects?" is an appropriate question, as all children can use what they have learned in the classroom to answer it. More important, all children can now answer application questions, such as "How do you know these are insects? Is a spider a type of insect? How is a fly similar to an ant? How are they different?" As teachers, giving information before application ensures that all children come to problem-centered discussions and activities with the baseline knowledge and vocabulary to participate actively and refine their learning.

Guided practice, then, is not synonymous with independent practice. Rather, it's really designed to help children develop deeper meanings of the words you've selected in a carefully scaffolded manner to make sure that any confusions or misconceptions have been resolved.

Step 4: Distributed Review

Once children have a firm grasp on the words that you teach, many opportunities must be provided to review these words, both initially and over time. These experiences should build deeper knowledge and involve children in independent activities, using what they've learned to learn more. In our work, we have found that children can learn these challenging words, but they are likely to lose them without regular review. Psychologists use the term *overlearning*, which refers to the practice of reviewing newly acquired words well beyond the point of initial mastery.

For example, you might include many new books in your classroom library on the topic of marine mammals, adding those that might be challenging for the children to read. They're likely to find these key words used again and again, and develop new knowledge on their own. We also make sure that we have placed the books that we've read together in the library for their continual review and rereading.

We place these key words on a pocket card or on the wall, under the title "Magic Words" so that children can use them in their independent activities. The list of magic words—words that are conceptually related to our topic—grows substantially throughout our work together, giving the children a sense of their progress and making them more word conscious—aware of the words around them. The words on the pocket chart provide more dynamic opportunities for learning than traditional "word walls," which too often become synonymous with "wallpaper"—seen but not remembered.

In contrast to daily review, we find that distributed review is more effective. This means that we will want to revisit these words at further points, sometimes a week or two later. In some cases, you might find that children might need more substantial review, whereas others need just a quick reminder or two. In our work, we try to cluster topics so that the next set of lessons might be on a topic that will include some of the words we have just taught. For example, we might focus on the topic of plants after we've completed our work on marine

---

IN THE CLASSROOM: REVIEW WITH "BRAINS-ON" SMALL-GROUP ACTIVITIES

Another way to reinforce vocabulary and conceptual learning is to engage children in small-group activities that expand upon and reinforce information they have gained during whole-group discussions. We think of these activities as "brains on" not just "hands on" because they are carefully planned to reinforce words and concepts rather than to focus just on a craft, a project, or skill practice. For example, children pantomime growing from a seed to a plant while the teacher narrates using the new vocabulary that children have learned: *"The spring rains sprinkle on our soil. Now the warm sun is shining and you are getting warm in the soil. Your roots start to grow downward and your shoots start reaching upward. You are germinating. Your new stem pokes through the soil. Your new leaves start unfurling and you grow. The sun keeps shining, the air blows around your stem and leaves, the rain moistens your soil, and you grow and grow and GROW!"* After the teacher describes this process, each child can take a turn to describe the life cycle of a plant as the teacher and a small group of children act out this process. Consider adding small-group activities that necessitate applying new concepts and vocabulary during investigations and play.

BUILDING HOME–SCHOOL CONNECTIONS: PRACTICE VOCABULARY WITH TAKE-HOME PICTURE CARD GAMES

One of the best ways to support children's vocabulary development is to make sure that children have many opportunities to practice using and applying the new words that they have learned. We have found that sending children home with topic-related picture cards and directions for a game encourages families to play together while reinforcing new words and concepts. Give children the opportunity to play card games at school before sending them home so that they can become experts, teaching them to family members. Here are several games that children love to play:

- **Picture Card Sorts.** Sort the pictures into two piles. Make one pile of cards that are related to the topic of study (e.g., "living things") and another pile of cards that are not related. Remember to discuss *why* each picture is sorted into each pile.
- **Picture Card Lotto.** This game requires four boards with 9 pictures on each board in a 3x3 grid, as well as 36 pictures to match the pictures on each board. Give each player a board. Place all picture cards face down in the center. On his or her turn, each player picks up a picture card. If it matches a picture on the player's board, he or she places it on the board covering the picture. If the picture does not match the board, the player puts it back, face down, where it was found. The first player to cover all pictures on his or her board yells, "Lotto!" and wins the game.
- **Picture Card Dominoes.** Create picture card dominoes with two side-by-side pictures. Each player starts with five dominoes. The rest are stacked faced down. The first player places a domino face up in the center. The second player plays a domino with a matching picture, lining it up so that the matching pictures on the two dominoes are touching. If a player does not have a domino with a matching picture, he or she draws from the stack until a domino with a matching picture is found and played. When one player has used up all of his or her dominoes, this player is the winner and the game ends.

Picture card dominoes for a study of scientific tools

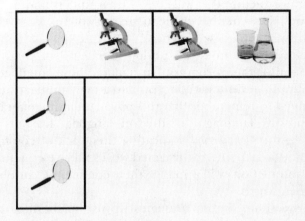

- **Picture Card Memory Game.** Send home two of each picture card. Place all picture cards face down in the center of the players. Each player picks two cards at a time and turns them over. If the cards match, *and the player can name the picture that is on both cards*, the player keeps the pair. If the cards do not match or the player cannot name the pictured objects, he or she puts them back, face down, where they were found. The game continues until no cards are left. The player with the most pairs of matching cards wins the game.

mammals. Children will have new opportunities to think about words such as *oxygen* and *carbon dioxide* in the context of a new kind of "living thing." Clustering topics in units like this allows you to naturally distribute the review of words over time.

Step 5: Monitoring Children's Progress

The only way we can be sure that children are learning is to regularly monitor their progress. If we can catch children's misconceptions about certain words or concepts, we can correct them right away. When misconceptions enter long-term memory, it's much harder to clear up any confusions or major problems.

Given how busy an average teacher's day is, we need to be efficient in how we monitor children's progress. It needs to be done quickly but accurately, to give you time to reteach. You'll also have to consider different modes or levels of understanding. For example, we find that some children can indicate their understanding of a word receptively; that is, they can identify a term if asked to point to a word or picture, or they can draw a picture that will convey their understanding. However, in some cases, they will not be able to use the word expressively, such as by using the word in a new sentence.

Therefore, sometimes we underestimate what children know when we monitor their progress, particularly those language learners who are grappling with new concepts and a new language at the same time. We need to remember that receptive language generally comes before expressive language. In addition, language learners are likely to go through a *silent period,* indicating their lack of comfort in trying out new words. Using the targeted words more frequently in your day-to-day interactions will enhance their confidence, and help them to try out new words.

Here are some simple strategies we use to monitor children's progress:

- **Every-pupil response techniques.** These are fun techniques that you can use to quickly monitor children's progress. We play a game called "Can you?" with the whole group, asking questions that call for a yes/no response, or thumbs up/thumbs down. For example, we'll say:
  - Can you see a *dolphin* in a fish bowl?
  - Can you find seaweed in the *ocean?*
  - Can you make a *manatee* fly?

Even such a quick exercise like this can tell us whether or not children have learned the key words. Also, you can use many variations on these ideas to give you a sense of children's level of understanding.

- **Record their descriptions of words and concepts.** Ask children to draw, drite (draw and write), or write about their descriptions of words and give examples of them. Let them be as creative as possible, and you can check their understanding by having them label terms in pictures or describe them verbally.
- **Small-group activities.** Some very simple games, such as word or picture bingo and concentration, can quickly identify children's understanding of new words. Some teachers will monitor children's progress while they are playing, using a checklist, to determine if there are problems or a need to review.

ADDITIONAL STRATEGIES FOR
PROGRESS MONITORING

Anecdotal Notes. Many teachers already have systems for keeping anecdotal notes on children's progress. Add vocabulary to these records. Jot down notes after a whole- or small-group lesson that is focused on your topic of study to track children who may or may not be participating fully.

Checklists. Keep a list of the vocabulary words that you are trying to teach and put a child's initials next to each word when you see or hear evidence that the child can use it. This can be done quickly at any time during the day. If certain vocabulary words have very few initials next to them, that might be a sign that most children in the classroom need more explicit instruction and practice opportunities for these words. On the other hand, if one child's initials rarely appear across the list of words, this child might need more individualized opportunities to practice and review new vocabulary with you.

Self-Monitoring. Researchers have found that children are good judges of whether or not they know a word's meaning. In fact, children's self-reported knowledge of a word's meaning and their actual knowledge when tested by adults were highly correlated. Children's responses to questions such as "Have you heard this word before?" and "Do you know what it means?" are likely to be accurate (see, for example, the Vocabulary Knowledge Scale; Wesche & Paribakht, 1996). This will give you some quick information on whether a child has learned a new vocabulary word.

Notice that these strategies are designed to better understand what children are learning. They are all informal, and can be included easily in your instructional repertoire. Yet at the same time, they are invaluable, giving you a roadmap for helping your children develop the vocabulary and concepts they will need to be successful in future learning.

Together, these five steps constitute an instructional regime that will help your children develop a rich vocabulary and conceptual knowledge base. The sequence is based on a careful selection of words, a deep and thorough explanation of their meanings, and lots of guided practice to ensure that students are on the right track, followed by independent and ongoing review. By the time you monitor progress, you should be proudly confident that students will be successful in learning because of your hard work.

IN THE CLASSROOM:
SELECTING CONTENT VOCABULARY

Every year, Ms. Hernandez's class discusses the weather during their morning meeting. They typically use words such as *sunny, rainy, cloudy, snowy, hot,* and *cold* to describe the weather conditions each day. This year, Ms. Hernandez decided to focus on content-rich vocabulary instruction. She used an instructional framework to guide her teaching that included thoughtful word selection, explicit instruction, guided practice, distributed review, and progress monitoring. This well-planned sequence of instruction, based on research evidence, ensured that all of her children build word and world knowledge in her classroom.

To choose words, Ms. Hernandez thought about the type of vocabulary you might encounter in a weather report, but also in literature when the author describes the setting. She focused on content words that help children to describe and discuss weather conditions: *breeze, blizzard, drizzle, fog, frost, flurries, hail, haze, humidity, hurricane, lightning, muggy, overcast, precipitation, showers, sleet, slush, temperature, tornado,* and *wind-chill.* Other challenging words that she used in these conversations included *advisory, climate, conditions, environment, forecast, map, meteorologist, observe, predict, report,* and *seasons.*

The most exciting results of the endeavor were the changes in children's conversations each morning—children eagerly anticipated discussing the weather, even asking their parents to check the weather report before school. They were excited to show what they had learned and began to use content vocabulary to describe their world:

Ms. Hernandez: What are the weather conditions that you observed on the way to school this morning?

Sophia: It was drizzling and overcast.

William: I asked my mom and the weather report is predicting showers the whole day!

Ms. Hernandez: Did anyone notice the temperature?

Ava: It's kinda warm and also muggy.

BUILDING HOME–SCHOOL CONNECTIONS:
TRY IT AT HOME

Another way to make connections between the words and concepts taught at school and children's homes is to ask children to explore a topic you are studying in their home environment. Here are some ways that teachers have encouraged children to extend their school studies by making discoveries at home:

Looking for Light. Ms. Allen's 2nd-graders are learning about light. She asked the children to explore their homes to look for all the light sources they could find in each room. She asked children to create a map of one room (e.g., kitchen) in their homes and then draw and label all of the light sources in that space.

Local Animals. The children in Christina's preschool class are learning about the animals that live in their local environment. She asked families to take children to the park to look for all of the animals (bigger animals such as squirrels and tiny animals such as mosquitoes) that they could find. Children were sent home with special local animal journals where they could draw pictures of all of the creatures they found.

Both teachers found that children were excited to share the words and concepts that they were learning at school when they were at home with their families. Children returned to school eager to describe their work on these projects with family members and to compare and discuss their findings with their friends.

A SELF-TEACHING APPROACH

Why is this approach so powerful? And how does it differ from other methods of vocabulary instruction? The answer is that when we teach words in meaningful clusters, it creates a self-teaching device that supports independent learning. In a sense, you are building a powerful schema for children that will enable them to attend better to new words, understand them, and retain them in a way that is easily accessible for future reference. For example, when we teach words such as *coyote, giraffe, leopard,* and *rhinoceros* in a meaningful semantic cluster, and teach children that they are all wild animals with a number of common features, children can begin to make the following generalizations about these animals:

- Wild animals are animals that live outside and away from people.
- Wild animals are not tame.
- Wild animals take care of themselves.
- Wild animals survive on their own in places that have the kind of weather they like and the kind of food they like to eat.
- Most wild animals are either herbivores or carnivores.

Now, here's where self-teaching comes into play: When we introduce children to a new word, such as *alligator* or *gorilla*, and we tell them that each refers to a wild animal, we find that children can make better generalizations and inferences about these new words. If a child learns that a python is a wild animal, for example, he or she is likely to make an inference that this animal is not tame, must take care of itself, lives outside and away from people, and so on. In other words, you have created a powerful frame of reference that allows children to easily slot new information, and make the generalizations on their own. These generalizations and developing concepts will help them enormously when they begin to read more complex text. By teaching words in a content-rich framework, we are providing children with a way of structuring their knowledge in ways that are efficient and accessible so they can become independent learners. In the final chapter, we'll share some of our strategies for assessing children's learning and the evidence for a content-rich approach.

In vocabulary acquisition, in particular, a small early advantage will grow into a much larger advantage as children begin to use these reasoning skills and generalizations to make more accurate inferences in complex text. The more words and knowledge networks you have, the more likely your guesses will be correct. This is the same process we all use to pick up new vocabulary throughout our lives. In this respect, then, it is only through this self-teaching device that children will be able to accumulate the estimated 15 words a day—or 5,000 words per year—with very different degrees of complexity and precision that children will need in order to successfully become career- and college-ready.

THINK ABOUT IT:
TEACHING WORDS AND CONCEPTS
THROUGHOUT THE DAY

How can you build content-rich vocabulary instruction into your day? At first, this might seem like more work, but we've found that this strategy of vocabulary instruction fits well with topics of study that are already being addressed in the classroom. Here are some questions that might help you to get started:

- Are there science topics that you already cover where you can focus more on vocabulary?
- Are there social studies topics that you already cover where you can focus more on vocabulary?
- Are there mathematics topics that you already cover where you can focus more on vocabulary?
- Can you teach vocabulary that is related to news or current events that you discuss in your classroom?
- Can you group sets of books that you already read aloud into a theme or topic and then teach vocabulary that you find across these texts?
- Can you teach vocabulary that is related to a genre of literature or writing that you are already discussing in your classroom (e.g., words related to poetry; words related to memoirs)?
- Can you teach vocabulary that is related to the art or music curriculum (e.g., types of instruments; styles of art)?

What we think about it:

Great words are everywhere! Across all content areas and topics that you teach, there are words that children need to learn in order to discuss their new ideas, discoveries, and knowledge. When you take the time to explicitly teach vocabulary in all parts of your curriculum, you support children's long-term learning. This is because children who know more vocabulary are better able to comprehend books that use those words. This, in turn, allows them to learn new concepts, and even more vocabulary, through their reading. So, your work on vocabulary instruction sets children up for school success!

4 Supporting Content-Rich Vocabulary Instruction Through Book Reading

Children learn words best when they are taught in meaningful contexts. Hearing new words in the context of fascinating stories and interesting new insights about their world is a natural context for vocabulary building. Good books also build content knowledge. Children are likely to learn a wide range of information during these book-reading activities. For example, notice how *The Very Hungry Caterpillar* (1981) delightfully captures the incredible metamorphosis of the caterpillar into a butterfly in Eric Carle's wonderful classic, weaving throughout this tale information about healthy foods and the days of the week. Book reading, therefore, is an ideal activity for supporting children's content-rich vocabulary and building a strong base of knowledge, which are critical for children's success in subsequent grades.

This emphasis on developing *knowledge through text* (Neuman & Roskos, 2012) represents one of the most notable shifts in the Common Core State Standards as compared to previous standards. In these new standards, you'll find a greater focus on informational text in science, social studies, and the arts in addition to traditional stories. In fact, guidelines for publishers have been modified to include over 50% of selections emphasizing informational reading (Coleman & Pimentel, 2012). Further, children are expected early on to become familiar with some of the genre features of informational text, which differ significantly from those of narrative stories. Consequently, our focus on content-rich vocabulary is well matched to meet these dual expectations in the new standards.

In this chapter, we'll describe reading materials to support these goals. First, we'll provide a rationale for including more informational texts in book reading, consistent with the Common Core State Standards. We'll focus on the differences between storybooks and informational texts and how these different genre features can support children's content-rich vocabulary. We'll then turn to describing how we use *text sets*—collections of resources from different genres—to support our vocabulary teaching sequence, as outlined in the previous chapter. Taken together, this will demonstrate how we can effectively teach children vocabulary and content knowledge simultaneously.

TYPES OF TEXTS

Thinking about the type of text is probably not at the top of your list when you select a book to read to children. Generally, teachers more often think about how a book might engage children's interest, or how it might support a particular theme of instruction. These certainly remain important considerations. However, it turns out that the type of text is also important because it affects how books are shared with children and what they may learn from them.

Let's take a simple example. When reading a book such as *Chicka Chicka Boom Boom* by Bill Martin and John Archambault (1991), with its delightful rhymes—"A told B and B told C, I'll meet you at the top of the coconut tree"—you're likely to try to help children play with its sounds and rhythms. You might emphasize the lyrical nature of the lines and encourage children to read along with you. At least in the first reading, you probably won't stop along the way, to avoid disrupting the flow of the reading. After the reading, it wouldn't make sense to retell the story, or recall events, as the point of the book is to have fun with the alphabet. And as many of us have experienced, there's no better book to help children remember their letters than this one.

Different types of books, therefore, can support and help us teach different skills. For example, the wonderful book *Corduroy* by Don Freeman (1976) can introduce children to the narrative structure of a well-constructed storybook. It begins with an opening that establishes the setting and the main characters. It has a complicating event, when little Corduroy loses a button on his overalls, which sets off a series of events. It follows by a resolution that is pleasing and satisfying to young children. It is an ideal book for helping children learn about narrative as a text type or genre. Children can often retell the story in vivid detail.

Therefore, in addition to the content of a book, we need to consider its genre (or text type), and what it can do to support children's learning. Although certainly not exhaustive, you'll see in the box "Common Text Genres and Features of Children's Books" some characteristics of different genres and the task-specific processes these text types tend to elicit. Studies (e.g., Price, van Kleeck, & Huberty, 2009)

COMMON TEXT GENRES AND FEATURES OF CHILDREN'S BOOKS

Alphabet Books

- Focus on letters of the alphabet
- Often include vocabulary words that begin with each letter
- Exemplars: *Chicka Chicka Boom Boom* by Bill Martin Jr., John Archambault, and Lois Ehlert; *Eating the Alphabet: Fruits and Vegetables from A to Z* by Lois Ehlert; *Animalia* by Graeme Base
- Are useful for teaching alphabet recognition and letter–sound correspondences
- May be topic focused (e.g., *Eating the Alphabet, Animalia*) and useful for building vocabulary for that topic

Rhyming Books

- Focus on sets of rhyming words and word play
- May include challenging vocabulary
- Typically focus on silly words more than a clear storyline
- Exemplars: *Green Eggs and Ham* by Dr. Seuss, *Jamberry* by Bruce Degen, *There Was an Old Lady Who Swallowed a Fly* by Simms Taback
- Are useful for promoting phonological awareness (i.e., the ability to distinguish sounds in oral language), which is a key early literacy skill

Storybooks

- Focus on telling a story with a setting, characters, and a plot
- Include a beginning, a conflict or problem, and an ending that resolves this issue
- May include challenging vocabulary and abstract language
- Exemplars: *Inch by Inch* by Leo Lionni, *Knuffle Bunny* by Mo Willems, *Corduroy* by Don Freeman
- Are useful for teaching story grammar (i.e., elements of a story) and literary language, and help children to learn about their own lives by exploring the experiences of others

have shown that these features of text can affect what children learn about language and literacy during shared book-reading activities.

Added to these familiar genres is the relatively new emphasis on informational text, or what is commonly called *expository text*. And this genre has some powerful features that make it especially useful for the development of content-rich vocabulary and background knowledge (see the box "Features of Informational Text"). For example, informational books tend to include technical words, and a larger proportion of high-frequency academic words as compared to narratives. They will use generic nouns and describe categorical features of things, such as "insects have three segments and six legs." Rather than

WOW Living Things: Insects
Teacher-Friendly Core Science Glossary

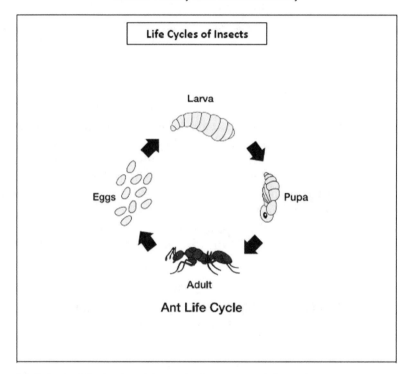

Adult: Insect fully developed; insect that has grown to full maturity.
Cocoon/Chrysalis: A protective case made by the insect larvae to keep it safe as it develops to adult maturity.
Egg: An object laid by the female insect from which the young develop.
Larva: The immature form of an insect (example: caterpillar, grub, or maggot).
Life Cycle: Stages of change that an insect goes through to reach adulthood.
Pupa: The inactive stage between the larva and adult in an insect.
Metamorphosis: The process that an insect goes through to transform from an immature form to an adult form.
Young: Offspring of an insect; new and not fully developed.

**FEATURES OF INFORMATIONAL TEXT
(BASED ON DUKE, 2000; DUKE & KAYS, 1998)**

- Purpose is to communicate information or factual content
- Frequent repetition of topic or theme
- Often in one of the following formats: compare/contrast, problem/solution, cause/effect
- Timeless verb constructions and generic noun constructions
- Technical vocabulary
- Provides definitions and classifications
- Graphic elements (e.g., diagrams, maps) to support the text

---

specific pronouns (e.g., *he* or *she*), you'll see the use of timeless verb constructions, such as "Cats are felines, and have excellent eyesight."

Informational books also differ from storybooks in the types of visual design features they include. Although both genres include picture scenes, the pictures in informational books are often intended to convey more technical or scientific kinds of information. They may include charts, graphs, and flow diagrams that will demonstrate causal relations, or tables that show comparisons or patterns. They may also rely on what Christine Pappas (1991) describes as "illustration extensions," including labels, captions, keys, and dialogue bubbles that provide explanations to aid in the interpretation of the text. Added

---

**BUILDING HOME–SCHOOL CONNECTIONS:
HOME JOURNALING**

Another way to support vocabulary learning with texts is to create your own informational texts. This can be done in the classroom by asking each child to contribute a page about a particular topic and then binding these pages together.

Another option is to include families in this process by sending home a journal with one child each night. The children can draw and write about what they learned at school concerning a particular topic. Each child takes

---

a turn to add to the class journal and brings it back to share with the group on the following day. Families love this activity because they get a glimpse into what their children have been learning about in school. Here are the instructions to include with the journal:

Dear Families,

For the next few weeks, we will be studying marine mammals at school. Each day, one child will bring home this Marine Mammal Journal and complete one page. Here are the instructions:

1. Take the journal out of the plastic baggie. Keep the baggie to return the journal in tomorrow.
2. Find the first blank page.
3. Draw a picture with lots of details to show something you learned at school today about marine mammals.
4. Write something you learned at school today about marine mammals.
5. Practice showing and reading your work so you are ready to tell your friends about it tomorrow.
6. Put the journal back in the baggie and make sure to return it to school in your backpack TOMORROW.
7. Thanks for your hard work on our class Marine Mammal Journal!

features such as indices and glossaries are also common features in informational text.

Book-sharing research has shown that these types of informational texts lend themselves to different types of conversational interactions with children than narrative stories. For example, a recent study found that teachers used more cognitively demanding talk when reading informational books compared to the more literal questioning in storybook reading (Price, Bradley, & Smith, 2012). Informational text also introduced more technical vocabulary as compared to the literary language of storybooks. Further, informational-book-sharing activities tend to elicit object-labeling routines (e.g., what's that?), in contrast to the more action-oriented routines in storybooks (e.g., what's happening?).

This means that when we engage children in book-sharing activities that involve multiple genres, we are likely to provide many different opportunities for interaction and responding. In addition, we are likely to build facility in understanding the different features of each type of text, and what they provide to readers and listeners. This may be especially important as children come to rely increasingly on informational text in later grades. At the same time, however, we certainly don't want the pendulum to shift too far in favor of one genre over another. Storybooks and predictable texts often bring information to life for young children and become meaningful to them in ways that informational books couldn't possibly capture. Therefore, we want children to become exposed to a healthy variety of different types of texts early on, all of which can support content-rich vocabulary instruction.

You can help the children in your class to make the most of informational texts by teaching the vocabulary and background knowledge they'll need. One way to develop children's vocabulary on a particular topic is to use text sets that include simple rhyming or predictable texts, storybooks, narratives (stories) that provide

THINK ABOUT IT:
WHICH TEXT GENRES ARE YOU USING?

Take a careful inventory of your classroom library and other children's book displays in the classroom.

- Are most books in the same genre?
- Do you provide books in a range of genres?
- Do you typically read aloud from only one genre?
- Do children have opportunities to read and listen to informational texts?
- Do you have texts from a variety of genres that address a single topic?

What we think about it:

The Common Core Standards put a particular emphasis on children's ability to read and learn from informational texts. So, teachers need to make certain that children are exposed to informational texts from a young age. One challenge of informational texts is that they typically include technical or academic vocabulary. Children need support from their teachers to learn these words and concepts so they can comprehend these books.

information, and informational texts. Reading many books on the same topic that utilize a similar set of vocabulary reinforces children's learning and supports their comprehension. So, if you don't have sets of books in your classroom, now is the time for a visit to your local library to stock up.

TEXT SETS

To support our goals, we have come to rely on text sets—collections of books that focus on a concept or a topic. For example, our most recent text set engaged children in learning about the life sciences, as a way of integrating reading and science instruction. Our intention was to spend 2 weeks on the topic, focusing on the content-rich vocabulary and the big ideas associated with the topic of "living things":

> ## BIG IDEAS FOR LIVING THINGS
>
> - Living things have life cycles.
> - Living things live in certain habitats based on their needs.
> - Living things have ways of protecting themselves.

Text sets are unified by the topic they explore. At the same time, they are differentiated by their genre and their format. The topic of flight, for instance, can be a focal point for a collection of books that could include a biography of the Wright brothers and an informational book on the basics of aerodynamics of flight. Notice in the following examples that we try to keep our text sets coherent—rather narrowly focused on a set of key ideas—to ensure that children will have repeated opportunities to hear and develop an understanding of a common set of words and concepts (see examples) throughout the readings.

Text sets are also organized to engage children with increasingly complex text. We do this by scaffolding children's experience with text, starting with more familiar genres before we introduce the less familiar informational genre. Using a recent topic about insects—which children just love to talk about—here's the sequence we used (see Appendix A for more examples):

- **Start with a predictable book.** Predictable books typically have a memorable rhyming or repetitive word pattern that enables children to anticipate words, phrases, and events in the story. Although we traditionally think of predictable books for their literary language, many of these books also include academic terms and vocabulary that children will need to learn in the subject areas. For example, we started with Eric Carle's *The Grouchy Ladybug* (1996), a delightful book about each hour in a lady bug's life and the different animals it runs into on its journey. The pages are layered so that the child can see the different times on the clock referred to on each page. In addition to the literary language, children are introduced to words such as *larva, pupa, molting, thorax,* and *abdomen,* all in the context of the predictable text. After rereading this book

SAMPLE TEXT SETS

(See Appendix A For Additional Text Sets)

Topic: The Water Cycle

Predictable: Greenfeld, E. (1999). *Water, water.* New York: HarperFestival.
Fiction: Arnold, T. (1998). *No more water in the tub!* New York: Puffin.
Informational (Narrative): Waldman, N. (2003). *The snowflake: A water cycle story.* Minneapolis, MN: Milbrook Press.
Informational (Expository): Strauss, R. (2007). *One well: The story of water on earth.* Tonawanda, NY: Kids Can Press.
Informational (Expository): Morgan, S. (2010). *Water for everyone.* North Mankato, MN: Sea to Sea Publications.

Topic: Objects in the Sky/Our Solar System

Predictable: Milgrim, D. (1997). *Here in space.* Mawah, NJ: Bridgewater Books.
Fiction: Dayrell, E. (1990). *Why the sun and the moon live in the sky.* New York: Sandpiper.
Informational (Narrative): Milbourn, A., & Davis, B. (2006). *On the moon.* London: Usborne Publishing.
Informational (Narrative): O'Connor, J. (2011). *Fancy Nancy stellar stargazer.* New York: Harper.
Informational (Expository): Gibbons, G. (1987). *Sun up, sun down.* New York: Sandpiper.

Topic: Emotions

Predictable: Snow, T., & Snow, P. (2007). *Feelings to share from A to Z.* Oak Park Heights, MN: Maren Green Publishing.
Fiction: Bang, M. (1999). *When Sophie gets angry really, really angry.* New York: The Blue Sky Press.
Informational (Narrative): Curtis, J. L. (1998). *Today I feel silly and other moods that make my day.* New York: HarperCollins.
Informational (Narrative): Freymann, S., & Elffers, J. (1999). *How are you peeling?: Foods with moods.* New York: Arthur A. Levine Books.
Informational (Expository): Aliki. (1986). *Feelings.* New York: Greenwillow Books.

several times, we find that children begin to remember and use these words in meaningful contexts.

- **Rhyming books.** Rhyming books are especially helpful for children to hear the distinctive sounds within these academic words. In addition, rhymes often act as a mnemonic device, helping us to remember key terms. For example, we use *Have You Seen Bugs?* (Oppenheim, 1996), which identifies all of the key characteristics of bugs in colorful rhymes, giving children a more vivid account of certain terms through language, more than specific features you might see in a photograph. For example:

  - But some bugs form a chrysalis or spin a fine cocoon,
  - Where abracadabra! They grow wide wings in a magical changing room.

- **Introduce storybooks.** Informally, we've come to call these books "genre-benders" because they serve as a very important middle ground between storybooks and informational texts. Nell Duke (2000), for example, calls them narrative-informational books. They provide information about the topic in a storybook format. These books also have fun with the topic, and give students a chance to meet interesting creatures in many new contexts. We read books such as *Anansi the Spider* (McDermott, 1972, 1993), the wonderful Ashanti tale, or *Aaaarrgghh! Spider!* (Monks, 2007), a book with an unusual premise about a spider who wants to be endeared as a family pet, told with lively cartoonish illustrations, and talk about how although spiders might look like insects, they really aren't (because they do not have six legs and three body segments). These types of books allow children to play with the topic, and provide wonderful opportunities for lively discussion. For example, we ask children, to their delight, "Why wouldn't you want a spider as a family pet? Wouldn't it be easier than having a dog or cat? Why wouldn't your house be an ideal place for a spider?" In many ways, you'll find opportunities to talk about different habitats in your conversation with children.

- **Informational books.** When children are engaged in learning about interesting things, they want to become more expert in the domain. "Insects," it turns out, is clearly one of those topics. This is the time we capture their interest and desire to learn more. We find that informational book reading at this point becomes deeper and more meaningful because children now have at least a beginning network of words and concepts from which to draw. For example, our students became fascinated in learning more about ants, and to understand more about these amazing little creatures, we read *The Life and Times of the Ant* (Micucci, 2006). This book goes into a lot of detail about how ants communicate, reproduce, and survive, and includes information on some predators of ants, such as the anteater and ant lion. It also looks back at the history of the ant, which evolved from wasps more than 100 million years ago. We find children so interested that they work with their teachers and assistants to use the classroom iPads to find videos of some of the insects described in the books. Further, these books have all the genre features we have come to associate with informational text, including diagrams, captions, and a glossary.

HOW TO SELECT BOOKS FOR TEXT SETS

You'll want to think carefully about putting your text sets together. When selecting books for your text sets, consider the following criteria:

- Books should include challenging vocabulary related to important concepts that stretch children's language. Children need to hear words that are outside of their day-to-day language.
- The information presented in the texts—the vocabulary and concepts—should be accurate and extend children's knowledge about the topic.
- Books should include a certain degree of overlap in vocabulary and concepts to support practice and review. In addition, when children hear the same words in multiple contexts, it builds their understanding of word meanings.
- Books should be challenging but achievable; read-aloud books can always be a grade level or two above children's current reading level.

BUILDING HOME–SCHOOL CONNECTIONS: SUPPORTING FAMILY VISITS TO THE LIBRARY

In addition to the text sets that are read in the classroom, teachers can support children in learning from texts at home. Here are several suggestions for extending and supporting content-rich shared book reading in children's homes:

- Make sure each child in your class has a public library card. Send home copies of your local library's application form for library cards.
- Take a class trip to the local public library, and make sure that each child knows how to select and check out books.
- For each topic of study in your classroom, look for titles on this topic that are owned by your local public library. Send home a list of recommended books for each topic of study.
- Also, send home a list of vocabulary words that parents can point out and explain to children when these words are encountered in a book.
- Visit your school library or create a classroom lending library where children can check out books that are related to your topic of study.

Combining genres in text sets gives children a rich opportunity to engage in learning the vocabulary, concepts, and information in many different contexts. Each of our text sets includes about five books to be read over a 2-week period, although the number of books and the time devoted to the topic can certainly be adjusted to meet your curriculum and your children's interests. This gives you opportunities to reread each text, which will provide further repetitions of these words and concepts. These text sets are the reading materials that we use to build children's vocabulary, following the teaching sequence described in Chapter 3.

APPLYING THE INSTRUCTIONAL REGIME TO TEXT SETS

It's spring, and Martha King's kindergarten class is about to start a 2-week unit on the topic of plants. She has gathered a good selection of predictable, narrative, and informational books (see Appendix A), all of which focus on a set of big ideas that are related to children's outcomes according to the literacy and science standards. She wants children to learn that:

- Plants are living things.
- Plants need sunlight and water to grow.
- Plants have important parts that help them live and grow.
- Plants adapt to different environments.
- Some parts of plants can be food for people and animals.

To accomplish these outcomes, Martha knows that she'll need to teach some words that reflect different types of plants. For example, given that flowering plants (such as a sunflower), cacti, and bushes need very different environments to grow and require different amounts of sunlight and water, they represent good exemplars to begin to compare and contrast patterns of growth and development in plants.

She'll then look through her books and select words that are essential to know and use when talking about plants. For example, here are some words that stand out when reviewing these books: *absorb,*

bark, bloom, branch, desert, fertilize, forest, fragrant, fruit, garden, ground, leaf/leaves, moist/moisture, petal, poisonous, pollen, ripe, roots, sapling, seed, seedling, spines, stem, sun/sunlight, support, texture, topsoil, trunk. From here, she will decide how to group these words into meaningful clusters to help children build knowledge networks. She often uses the "Goldilocks principle" in selecting the number of words to teach: Too many words taught at one time can be overwhelming; too few, on the other hand, might underutilize instructional time—the amount needs to be "just right." At the end, she decides to cluster words on the basis of the concepts she is trying to teach. For example, words such as *roots, seedlings, seeds, leaves,* and *petals* clearly describe the parts of the plant, and seem like a natural to go together in a lesson.

At the same time, she'll also select some "challenge" words. These are words that have an important conceptual base in science—*carbon dioxide, oxygen, photosynthesis*—and are interesting to talk about. It is important to introduce children to these concepts early on, knowing that subsequent learning progressions over time will further deepen children's understandings. Notice here, however, that because of the complexity of the concepts, she doesn't pick too many challenge words. This will give children the amount of time needed to dig deeper in developing these concepts.

With the text set determined and the words selected, Martha's ready to begin. On the first day of instruction, she plans to introduce children to the words *sunflower,* a bright and memorable type of flower, and *grass,* something that is common in their environment. She selects these exemplar words to emphasize the differences between plants and to create an interesting problem for the children to consider: "Did you ever wonder why grass is so short and why a sunflower is so tall? They look very different, but some things about them must be the same. Let's see if we can figure this out." Before reading the book, she'll show a picture of each, and provide a child-friendly definition. Then she'll read the first book in the text set, *The Tiny Seed* by Eric Carle (1987). Like so many of Eric Carle's books, this story helps children learn about the life cycles of nature. The text is quite poetic, yet the language is clear enough for young listeners or readers to understand. It starts off following one little seed, which is planted and watered and eventually turns into a towering sunflower. When it's mature, it produces more seeds, all of which are planted and turn into sunflowers of their own. Kids love the subtle word play while they learn about the way that seeds become plants, and how more seeds are produced. The predictability of the text helps children read along. She'll read the book straight through the first time, without stopping, to focus on the continuity in the language of the text.

After the reading, Martha says, "Let's talk about the sunflower. Do you ever wonder how one might grow?" Pointing again to the pictures, she describes the process: "First, there's a seed, and then roots reach down into the soil. Next, the plant pushes up to the top of the soil and leaves begin to grow. Last, there is a plant growing in the sun!" Notice how she provides an explicit explanation (rather than asking open-ended questions) in the beginning of the topic. Later on as children build knowledge, Martha will begin to turn control over to the children. In this case, after her description, she encourages the children to act out each stage of the growth process.

All together, the lesson takes about 12 minutes to enact. On the next day, she'll reread the same story, focusing this time on how grass and sunflowers are similar in their needs, and how they are different. Contrasts and comparisons help children to develop more nuanced understandings of these words and the concepts that underlie them. Children are likely to be more conscious of the words they've heard the day before. She'll also more explicitly introduce additional words associated with the plants. Rereading the predictable book, the first in the text set, will provide a vivid reminder to children of the words in their discussions. Predictable books act almost like a mnemonic device to help children remember these words.

In the next set of lessons, Martha's text set is designed to develop the concepts that she's identified in greater depth. She introduces vocabulary for different types of plants—cactuses—and the kind of habitats that support these types of plants. She reads a variation of a wonderful classic—*Cactus Soup* (Kimmel & Huling, 2004), the familiar "Stone Soup" story with a Mexican flavor, with added tamales and peppers, which has predictable elements, but with a stronger emphasis on story. After reading, she'll ask children to compare and contrast the different habitats that cacti, sunflowers, grass, and bushes are likely to experience. Each time children do this, they are making subtle distinctions between the meanings of the words, which adds to their comprehension. It also encourages children to use these words in multiple contexts, and to begin to express themselves more actively in discussions.

Because Martha is planning for the children to set up a garden, toward the end of the week she introduces them to the book *City Green*

(DiSalvo-Ryan, 1994). This is a realistic story about how young Mary, Miss Rosa, and their neighbors transform a vacant lot into a community garden of flowers and vegetables, with watercolor, pencils, and crayon illustrations that beautifully capture the transformation of the lot. The story features information about the kinds of food and nutrients plants will need in order to grow, introducing the concepts of *carbon dioxide* and *photosynthesis* in an interesting and relevant way. In this book, the children will once again hear how roots, stems, and leaves help the plant to find food to grow. Hearing these words in a new context will increase the frequency of exposure, and give children opportunity for practice, enhancing their depth of processing.

As the next week progresses Martha thinks that it's time for something a bit more light-hearted. She selects the book *How Groundhog's Garden Grew* (Cherry, 2003), which is about a little squirrel that discovers a groundhog eating veggies from a neighbor's garden, and decides to teach him a lesson. Now that Martha and the children's plans have been put in place for planting their garden, this seems like an ideal book about growing a vegetable garden. In addition, the author has included an amazing amount of information about how to garden in this story, with illustrations that are compelling for the children.

By this time in their study of the topic, toward the eighth day in the 10-day schedule, children have been introduced to all the words that Martha has selected. Now, it will be a matter of helping children to use these words in ways that make them their own. She'll find that although they have a bit of difficulty using the word *photosynthesis* (which she teaches by clapping each syllable together), they have developed an overall conceptual framework and understanding of the meaning that underlies the word. As the days go by, the lesson time takes a bit longer, as there is now much more discussion about the topic. Martha has given them the background from which to ask questions and she find that other children are able to provide many answers.

Notice throughout the sequence of activities the "gradual release of responsibility" on Martha's part. At the beginning of the topic, she engages in a good deal of explicit instruction, providing a foundation for children's learning. As they develop a better understanding of terms and the topic, she relinquishes a certain amount of control to support children's increasing independence. It becomes evident in the class discussions, which increasingly look like interactive conversations.

The final book in the text set is *Plant Secrets* (Goodman, 2009), an interesting informational book that informs as it describes the secret each plant holds. The author describes the plant cycle, how different plants look when they mature, the elements needed by each plant to grow, and the secret each plant holds. The vocabulary and concepts have all been described in earlier books in the text set, providing a wonderful opportunity for review and further practice. In addition, however, Martha will highlight the differences in this type of book from the others, showing children how to use the glossary and

RUBRIC FOR ASSESSING TOPIC KNOWLEDGE THROUGH DRAWING, WRITING, AND DICTATING

Ask each child to draw and write about the topic that the class has been investigating. Encourage children to:

- Add as many details as you can to your drawing to show what you know
- Label or write about your drawing to show what you know
- Tell me about your work (don't forget to help children write down their chosen words)

Use the following rubric to keep track of each child's progress:

Needs Additional Instruction	Developing Knowledge	Secure Knowledge
The child draws, writes, or dictates limited information about the topic, even with adult support and prompting	The child draws, writes, or dictates some information about the topic with adult support and prompting.	The child independently draws, writes, or dictates information about the topic.
The child draws, writes, or dictates few or no key concepts, even with adult support and prompting.	The child draws, writes, or dictates some key concepts with adult support and prompting.	The child independently draws, writes, or discusses many key concepts.
The child draws, writes, or dictates few or none of the new vocabulary that has been taught, even with adult support and prompting.	The child draws, writes, or dictates some new vocabulary that has been taught with adult support and prompting.	The child independently draws, writes, or dictates many new vocabulary words that have been taught.

pointing to the diagrams on various pages. Because children now have a strong background, the book adds a special value, introducing them to some of the genre features that they are likely to encounter in the future. Further, the children are now taking on independent learning, engaging in discussions with one another on the topic.

On the final day of instruction, Martha asks the children to draw a picture—to use symbols and other graphic representations to show what they've learned about plants. In this case, she gives them an unlined paper folded in four parts, and asks them to draw and write how plants grow. She encourages them to use developmental spelling to identify terms, and provides additional paper for them to describe how the various terms are related. She will score each paper on a scale of 1 to 3, with 1 being "needs additional instruction," 2 being "developing knowledge," and 3 being "secure knowledge" of words and concepts. She'll use this as a method to monitor children's progress, and to determine individual differences in the pace of learning. She'll plan for additional lessons for those who need it.

By the time the topic is over—and in this case, while the classroom instruction will move on to another topic children are just beginning to watch their garden grow—they will have learned over

50 new words and new concepts that are fundamental to environmental science, and these words and concepts will be connected in a way that builds a knowledge network. These knowledge networks are important because they have established these words and concepts into long-term memory, making retrieval of information more automatic. When children encounter these words in written contexts as they develop their reading skills, they will have the conceptual apparatus to understand what they mean, enabling them to engage in self-teaching while reading. By using text sets and carefully selecting words that are challenging to children, Martha has provided them with opportunities to engage in more in-depth learning. She has

THINK ABOUT IT: MAKE YOUR OWN TEXT SET

Select a topic of study that you will soon be addressing in your classroom. Can you find five or six books that address the concepts you want children to learn? As you select these books, use the following checklist as a guide. If your answers to the following are all "yes," then you are ready to get started!

Yes	No	Checklist for Text Sets
		Are all books appropriate for reading aloud (i.e., more challenging than books children can read independently)?
		Are books selected from a variety of genres?
		Is the information about your topic accurate in all books, even in storybooks?
		Do the books include challenging vocabulary that is important for your topic of study?
		Are the same vocabulary words found across multiple texts?

What we think about it:

Following these guidelines will help you to select a great set of read-aloud texts. Using a variety of books, from a variety of genres, helps to keep children interested and engaged over a longer period of time. It also has another key benefit: naturally occurring opportunities for practice and review. Each time you begin a new book, children will have another chance to engage with the concepts and vocabulary they are learning. This repetition helps them to retain the vocabulary they have learned and to deepen their knowledge of word meanings as they encounter the same words in new contexts.

given them the background knowledge and the academic vocabulary so that they are now capable of engaging in rich discussions that will extend their understandings further.

CONCLUSIONS

You'll find that text sets provide an extraordinary opportunity to teach words in meaningful contexts. Thinking about the genre of book helps us to understand how a book's structure can act as a scaffold for learning. When text sets are thoughtfully developed, they can help to support the instructional regime by providing repeated practice and review of new words. They can enable children to understand subtle differences in the meanings of words in these new contexts, building not only breadth but also depth of word knowledge. Further, they can teach children a great deal about genre features, which will become increasingly important in the Common Core State Standards. What is striking about text sets is that they allow us to build important background knowledge and vocabulary, as well as the characteristics of genre that will be essential to comprehending text in later grades. Early on, you are helping children to begin the process of developing knowledge networks that are coherent, meaningful, and accessible when they go to read more complex texts.

5 Grouping for Vocabulary Instruction

As most teachers recognize, there is an organizational rhythm in successful instruction in early childhood classrooms. You can feel it when you walk in a classroom. You'll hear the gentle tones of conversation as children are listening to a story in a whole-group setting, the busier and more active interactions during small-group time, and the mixed cacophony of louder and softer voices when children are engaged in independent explorations and individual work time. Organizing your classroom for instruction is both an art and a science, for it recognizes how children's development is integrally tied to their dispositions for learning and learning outcomes.

In this chapter, we'll focus on techniques for successfully organizing vocabulary instruction, building on the principles we've described in previous chapters. We'll first give you a rationale for why the organization of instruction is especially important in the age of Common Core Standards. We'll take a look at the most typical ways we group for instruction and describe both the benefits and the challenges of each configuration. We'll then describe ways in which you can take advantage of each organizational structure, maximizing not only children's natural desire to learn, but their ability to effectively communicate their ideas with others.

ORGANIZING VOCABULARY INSTRUCTION IN THE AGE OF COMMON CORE STANDARDS

Providing opportunities for children to actively communicate has always been a primary focus in early childhood. However, the Common Core Standards clearly up the ante. Focusing particularly on the speaking and listening standards, children are expected to fully participate in collaborative conversations with others, and to follow the social rules associated with good conversations. For example, they are expected to listen carefully to others, and to not interrupt someone in the middle of a sentence. They are to take turns speaking, and to extend the conversation rather than divert the discussion to a new topic. Further, they are expected to be able to ask and answer questions to clarify their thinking on something they may not understand, and to express themselves and their ideas clearly and articulately.

STANDARDS IN EARLY CHILDHOOD: SPEAKING AND LISTENING

Comprehension and Collaboration

- Participate in collaborative conversations with diverse partners about topics and texts
- Follow agreed-upon rules for discussions (e.g., taking turns at speaking)
- Continue a conversation through multiple exchanges
- Confirm understanding of a text read aloud by answering and asking questions

Presentation of Knowledge and Ideas

- Describe familiar people, places, and things
- Add drawings or other visible displays to descriptions to provide additional detail
- Speak audibly and express thoughts, feelings, and ideas clearly

COMMON CORE COLLEGE AND CAREER READINESS ANCHOR STANDARDS FOR SPEAKING AND LISTENING

Comprehension and Collaboration

1. Prepare for and participate effectively in a range of conversations and collaborations with diverse partners, building on others' ideas and expressing their own clearly and persuasively.
2. Integrate and evaluate information presented in diverse media and formats, including visually, quantitatively, and orally.
3. Evaluate a speaker's point of view, reasoning, and use of evidence and rhetoric.

Presentation of Knowledge and Ideas

4. Present information, findings, and supporting evidence such that listeners can follow the line of reasoning and the organization, development, and style are appropriate to task, purpose, and audience.
5. Make strategic use of digital media and visual displays of data to express information and enhance understanding of presentations.
6. Adapt speech to a variety of contexts and communicative tasks, demonstrating command of formal English when indicated or appropriate.

Clearly, these standards represent a tall order, especially for those of us who work with young children. However, their intention is important: to highlight the reciprocity of the language processes (speaking and listening vocabulary) and literacy development. When children are engaged in quality conversations that require them to ask and address information, it promotes vocabulary development. Therefore, the more we can provide opportunities for these behaviors to take place, the greater the likelihood that children will use and extend their developing word knowledge.

We need to consider how the organization of instruction may optimize these opportunities. Each organizational pattern—whole group, small group, and individual work time—has some unique strengths that we need to build on. Similarly, each has weaknesses, which means that there are times when some skills might be better taught and practiced in one organizational configuration over another. By identifying their strengths and weaknesses, we can begin to use grouping patterns more intentionally to further our goals to meet these challenging standards.

Whole-Group Instruction

The use of whole-group instruction in classrooms has been widely debated. There are those who decry all whole-group instruction, whereas others are more sanguine about its uses (Bowman, Donovan, & Burns, 2000). Clearly, however, there is broad consensus that reliance on whole-group instruction as the primary mode of instruction is neither appropriate nor optimal for language development and vocabulary learning.

Studies do show, however, that whole-group instruction can be highly effective in creating a sense of community in the classroom (Clark, Kirschner, & Sweller, 2012). It can provide a shared context for conversations, learning from one another, and hearing diverse perspectives. It can be an ideal setting for introducing new topics and concepts that the whole class will be exploring in different ways.

Particularly for vocabulary development, whole-group experiences can build a language for learning that is essential for further investigations. Think about the special power of introducing a favorite topic, such as insects, to the whole group, focusing on the common characteristics of these fascinating creatures. Then consider how sharing a book together before dispersing to individual work stations or activities allows children to build on the words and concepts they've just heard. In some very important ways, you are helping to level the playing field when you introduce these ideas in whole-group settings. You are giving all of your children opportunities to build background knowledge that can be used later on. You are providing them with the foundation for later learning.

STRATEGIES FOR SHARED BOOK READING IN WHOLE-GROUP SETTINGS

Sometimes it can be difficult to hold young children's attention during shared book reading in whole-group settings. Here are some tips for helping children to stay engaged when you read aloud.

During All Shared Book-Reading Times

- Before beginning, make sure that children are sitting so that they can all see the pictures.
- Before beginning, make sure that children are sitting with enough personal space so that they don't bump or bother each other during the book reading.
- Read with enthusiasm. Children take their cues about what is exciting and special from their teachers. Let children know through your tone of voice and body language that read-alouds are an important and enjoyable time for learning.
- Keep it short and sweet. Young children cannot sit for too long without getting restless.

- Try not to stop and correct every minor behavior infraction. For example, if a child lies down, looks out the window, or calls out a comment, try to keep going and maintain the group's focus on the book.
- Support children's comprehension as you go. Stop briefly to explain word meanings using child-friendly definitions or to reiterate important ideas or key points in the plot.

Predictable Books

- Read the same book multiple times so that children get to know the pattern.
- Encourage children to chant along with a rhyme or repeating phrase.
- Let children guess what will come next based on the predictable pattern.

Fiction and Narrative-Informational Books

- Use drama. Create voices for different characters and read with enthusiasm.
- Create suspense. Make sure that children are aware of the conflict or problem and that they listen for how it is resolved.

Informational Books

- Read to answer specific questions. Have children generate questions and then see if together you can find the answers in a book.
- Fact check. Point out words and concepts that children have already learned: "Hey everyone, we already know all about that! Let's check if this book has got it right!"

Here's what can be problematic in whole-group settings. They can get too long. Too often we have watched children squirm when the whole-group lesson drags on. We have also seen children act passively, bored and uninvolved in learning, when they are *talked to* rather than *engaged with*. Furthermore, we have often seen how administrative details (e.g., lunch monies, attendance, interruptions from the office) can derail lessons by shifting the focus away from the children. Pretty soon, off-task behaviors begin, the pacing of the lesson slows down, and children become less actively engaged in the material.

Rather, whole-group experiences should represent a joyous coming together of community; they should be spirited and lively in nature.

Generally, whole-group lessons should last only about 15 to 20 minutes (at most) and give children an energy boost to move on to other activities that are related to your topics of interest. Group time should be a time to learn together, not a place to compete for the correct response.

There are certain types of engagement patterns that support these goals. For example, choral responses and choral reading promote a sense of community. Encouraging children to respond to your cues, using a call-and-response technique, helps you maintain a brisk pace for learning that can be energizing for your eager young children. Using every-pupil response techniques with simple hand motions can allow all children to participate at the same time. Pantomiming or group games, such as "freeze when I say the magic word," are wonderful ways to support active listening and engagement.

IN THE CLASSROOM:
EVERY-PUPIL RESPONSE GAMES

Thumbs Up, Thumbs Down

During whole-group times, we can give children opportunities to practice something new they have learned by taking a poll of the group. Say, "I'm going to tell you something. If you agree that I'm saying something right, give me a big thumbs up. If you think that I'm saying something wrong, give me a thumbs down. Are you ready?" In one classroom where the children were learning about endangered species, the dialogue was as follows:

Teacher: We call a species *endangered* when we are concerned that it might go extinct.
Children: Thumbs up.
Teacher: You're right. So, that must mean that dogs are an endangered species.
Children: Thumbs down.
Teacher: How about kittens?
Children: Thumbs down.
Teacher: Deer?
Children: Thumbs down.
Teacher: You're right. There are a lot of all of those animals, so they are not considered endangered.

Ready, Set, Show!

Some teachers hand out small whiteboards, so that children can draw or write their responses and then hold them up. An example interaction is as follows:

Teacher: I'm thinking of a shape and I want you to draw it on your boards, but don't show anyone. Then, when I say "go," we are all going to hold up our boards at the same time. Are you ready? (children nod agreement)

Teacher: I'm thinking of a two-dimensional shape that has two pairs of parallel lines. One pair is longer and the other pair is shorter. This shape also has four vertices and they are all right angles like the corner of a page in a book. (children draw rectangles)

Teacher: Okay. Ready, set, show! (children hold up their whiteboards)

Teacher: Great job. Now can you all tell me the name of the shape that you drew?

Children: Rectangle!

These types of responses are the cognitive building blocks for more complex responses that occur in small groups or peer-assisted learning activities. They are designed to provide a risk-free environment for all children to participate. Contrast these patterns, for example, with the more typical pattern—asking children specific questions during whole-group time. Generally, here's what happens: Some children will raise their hands to respond; others do not. You are often left to guess why some did not respond. In other words, did they not know the answer? Are they merely reticent to say anything in front of a group because their answers might be incorrect? Are they disengaged? Any or all of these concerns may be at work. And then there is always the problem of what to do about the student who never raises his or her hand.

It is for these reasons that we use whole-group activities as a communal, noncompetitive setting to create an opportunity to introduce new words and share expertise in a way that supports our group as a community of learners. However, this does not mean that we can't support higher-level thinking in whole-group settings. There are some fun ways to create open-ended responses that engage the whole group, as discussed in the accompanying In the Classroom feature.

IN THE CLASSROOM:
TIME FOR A CHALLENGE— SUPPORTING OPEN-ENDED RESPONSES IN WHOLE-GROUP SETTINGS

Once her students have learned a lot about the words and concepts for a topic of study, Ms. Robertson engages them in open-ended conversations during whole-group time. She refers to these discussions as "time for a challenge" and presents topics that encourage children to use their knowledge to debate key ideas that have been studied. During a study of insects, Ms. Robertson had the following conversation with her students:

Ms. Robertson: Here's a challenge for you. Is a spider an insect? When you share your ideas, make sure to provide evidence to support your opinion.

Caleb: Yeah. A spider's an insect 'cause a spider's small and it can protect itself by biting you.

Avery: Yeah, but a spider's got eight legs, you know. Insects have six legs, so it can't be one.

Nora: Ms. Robertson, how many body segments does a spider have? It's gotta have three to be an insect.

Ms. Robertson: I think most spiders have two segments.

Nora: Well, then I think it's not an insect because it doesn't have enough segments.

Caleb: So maybe it looks like an insect but it's not really one.

Carrie: So a spider is some other type of bug but it's not, like, an actual insect.

Ms. Robertson: Wow! You guys really know how to think about the evidence to answer my challenging questions. You're right. Spiders are not insects, they're a type of creature called arachnids. Can you say *arachnid*?

Class: Arachnid.

Mr. Robertson: Good thinking.

BUILDING HOME–SCHOOL CONNECTIONS: USING WHOLE-GROUP TIME FOR SPECIAL GUESTS

Children's family members can be an important resource for specialized knowledge on topics that you are studying. Learn about what parents do for a living and their hobbies and invite them in to help children deepen their knowledge on specific topics of study. In particular, family members can help children to learn about real-life applications of the words and concepts that are learned in school. Here are some examples of wonderful family projects that have supported children's content learning:

- Yasmine's mother is a radiology technician. When the class was studying the human body, she came in and explained about some of the different technologies that she uses in her job that allow us to see inside the human body. Children enjoyed examining magnetic resonance imaging (MRI) scans and X-rays to figure out which bones they could see.
- Becky's grandfather is an avid gardener. Each summer, he grows herbs and vegetables in a local community garden plot. In the fall, Becky's father helped the children learn about plant growth and development, as well as healthy foods, by bringing in vegetables from his garden and answering children's questions.

(Continued)

> • Emma's mother is an architect. When the class was learning about three-dimensional shapes, she brought in some physical models of buildings as well as design software that shows three-dimensional views of a project. Children were excited to see a real-life application of the geometry vocabulary that they were learning.

Nevertheless, whole-group time does not easily lend itself to individual responses, and you will probably want to keep such time relatively brief, so that children do not have to sit for too long. There are many activities throughout the day that enable us to help children develop their individual ideas and express their thoughts more clearly. However, whole-group time should be a gathering in which we celebrate our work as a team together.

Small-Group Instruction

Instructing children in small groups can be a special pleasure because it allows you to get to know them in a way that is simply impossible in whole-group settings. You can better understand how an individual child performs on a task and how he or she interacts with other children. You can also provide richer corrective feedback when there are misunderstandings, and support children in asking and answering questions for clarification.

For vocabulary learning, small-group instruction is perhaps the most important context for developing the words that you have introduced in the whole-group setting. This is a key time for guided practice. In small groups, it is important to encourage children to use the words that they are learning, and for you to accept (in many cases) their approximations of word meanings and concepts to refine their understandings. For example, after talking about the word *echolocation* in the whole-group setting, one child said "elocution," with the teacher responding, "Yes, they sound rather similar, but the word actually is *ec-ho-lo-ca-tion*," stretching the sounds as she says the word, "the sensory sounds used by the dolphin that we talked about today in our group meeting."

To be most effective, however, small-group instruction needs careful planning and organization. Randomly organized groups that

merely respond to classroom management problems don't take advantage of the special opportunities that small groups provide to teachers. Rather, you might consider the following guidelines in establishing small groups.

Consider the size of the group: Generally, small groups are no longer small when they exceed six children. Breaking the entire class into two groups with half of the children working with an assistant or parent and the other half with the teacher doesn't break down the group in a way that supports vocabulary-learning goals. Groups with more than six children do not allow for the kind of interactive discussions and conversations that are at the heart of guided practice. With six or fewer children, you have the opportunity to focus your attention on both the group and the individual children within it.

The purpose of the activity. The size of your group will necessarily vary by the purpose and scope of the activity. For example, Lesley Morrow and her colleagues (Morrow, 1988) found that reading a book to a small group of three or four children promoted greater engagement and comprehension than reading a book on a one-to-one basis. In other words, the small-group activity sparked the kinds of collaborative conversations that are indicative of the speaking and listening standards in the Common Core. In these small groups, children talked to each other as well as to the adult, asking story-related questions and hearing responses by everyone participating. In the case where one or two children do not offer responses, the teacher can specifically ask the child the word's meaning, and can explain it in greater detail. In another activity, however, where we had children explore "blubber" by donning gloves and putting their hands in Crisco, and then describe all the "gooey words" they could think of, we had a more spirited engagement with six children than the much smaller group of three. Therefore, the nature of the activity should determine the specific number of children in the group.

Planned grouping. Consider how you plan your grouping patterns. For example, too often children are selected into small groups based on the ones who raise their hands first to participate, or run to an activity based on their interest. Sometimes this will mean that some children will never get the opportunity to participate in an activity. Rather, small-grouping patterns should be flexible and intentional. Flexible means that the

groupings should change, so that some children are not necessarily in the same group over extended periods of time. Intentional means that there is a careful coordination of the type of instruction and the needs of the individual students. Sometimes children can be grouped on the basis of needing additional time for instruction. One teacher, for example, formed a small group of six children to play a game of ocean bingo, recognizing that these children had some difficulty with identifying and sorting ocean mammals from other ocean creatures.

Other times, you will want to intentionally form heterogeneous groups, involving children with varying skill levels in small-group activities, knowing that children learn from one another. Still other times, you might form groups on the basis of working on a particular aspect of a topic. For example, in an investigation about shapes and dimensions, one group studied the surface textures of particular objects; another group measured their circumferences and compared them; and a third examined the multiple purposes of the objects and what they could be used for. These activities were best accomplished in small groups where children could explore and ask questions, and then come together as a community of experts to the whole group with much new information.

Needless to say, you will want to consider the composition of your small groups. Two children who have difficulty with one other will need to be in separate groups. Therefore, in planned groups, you'll need to consider the purposes of the activities as well as the personalities and skill levels of the children in these groups.

Managing small groups. Let's face it: It's often difficult to capture the undivided attention of 18 to 25 or more children at one time. No matter how good you are at management, all you need is that one child to be off task, and your instruction is interrupted. In small groups, you don't have these kinds of management difficulties, making it an ideal time to focus on extending the instruction that you introduced in whole group. Children will feel that they are being listened to and that they are important, especially if you can give them your undivided attention. Therefore, these are the times when you want to help them ask questions and hear their answers about key details, and when you want to informally probe a child's knowledge to make sure he or she understands. You can also informally ask questions and quickly determine if several of the children understand the meaning of the words that you have introduced. These types of interactions are possible in

ADDITIONAL STRATEGIES FOR ORGANIZING SMALL GROUPS

Work-Station Rotation

In this organizational strategy, small groups of children rotate through a series of work stations that the teacher has designed. Most of these stations include activities that children can work on independently or with a partner. The teacher stays at one work station and works with each small group as it comes to the area.

Time	Station 1 (with teacher)	Station 2	Station 3	Station 4
10:00–10:15	Group 1	Group 2	Group 3	Group 4
10:15–10:30	Group 2	Group 3	Group 4	Group 1
10:30–10:45	Group 3	Group 4	Group 1	Group 2
10:45–11:00	Group 4	Group 1	Group 2	Group 3

Must Do and Choice

This strategy is motivating for children because it combines required work stations with the opportunity for children to make their own choices. Children are given a checklist with the required work stations that they will need to visit over the course of the day. There are also optional stations (e.g., see the insert on discovery centers on p. 106 of this chapter) that children can select. Children can choose their own order for getting work done, checking off requirements as they do them. The teacher helps the children to make decisions about where to go next in order to ensure that all work is completed in the allotted time period.

MUST DO		CHECKLIST
Discovery Center		☐
Science Journals		☐

Choice		
Dramatic Play		☐
Block Area		☐
Library		☐

Jigsaw

Just like a jigsaw puzzle, where each piece has a different but important role to play, in a classroom jigsaw, each small group does one small but important part of a larger project. In this strategy groups work independently, but the resulting project or activity is interdependent. The teacher moves around the room and helps each small group as necessary. In a 1st-grade classroom where children were learning about marine mammals, each small group had the responsibility of learning about one type of mammal (see accompanying table) and then creating a poster to present to the rest of the class. Together, the posters would form a Marine Mammal Museum, which would hang in the hallway for other classes to see.

Group 1	Group 2	Group 3	Group 4
Seals	Whales	Dolphins	Walruses

the less stressful small group, as opposed to putting children on the spot in the large-group setting. In this sense, what you are doing in small-group instruction is digging deeper into the word meanings and concepts that you've introduced in large-group settings.

Small groups, therefore, can encourage more personal and positive interactions between you and your children and the children themselves. They will often help even the shyest children "give it a go." This is especially important for those young English language learners who are not quite yet comfortable in front of a large group. You will get to know

BUILDING HOME–SCHOOL CONNECTIONS: USING SMALL-GROUP TIME TO SHARE LEARNING WITH FAMILIES

In the past, sharing work with parents meant bulletin board displays or sending work home. Now, more and more, teachers and children are using technology to share work with families. Here are some suggestions for small-group opportunities to reinforce vocabulary that can be incorporated into a classroom blog or website:

- Create a (password-protected!) class blog. Children can take turns as the weekly blogger, where their job is to share important concepts that the class has learned over the course of a week. Family members are then able to keep up digitally with the learning in the classroom.
- Take photos of the children at work. Each week, one group of children can record audio files to explain the photos. Support children in learning their new vocabulary as they describe their learning. Post photos and audio files on the class blog or website for families.
- Rather than a paper book, create an e-book. (Note: Although you can use more sophisticated technology to do this, you can also create an electronic "book" that is a PowerPoint presentation.) Children can write and draw about a topic of study as they would in a journal. Combine each child's slides and post the book on your website or email it to families.

more about your children—their likes and dislikes, what makes them laugh, what favorite activities they enjoy, and how you can build on their unique strengths and interests.

At the same time, small-group instruction is not without its challenges. It's difficult to keep all children actively engaged in productive work. More often than not, children who are not working with you are likely to be working below their challenge levels; further, some students may be asking "When is it my turn?" In addition, the timing for small-group work must be very carefully orchestrated to ensure that all children have an equal opportunity to participate in the activities. Some children also have difficulty with transitioning from one activity to another, which may take up precious time. That said, once your students get into a routine for small-group instruction, many of these difficulties are no longer a problem.

Guiding children's learning and practice in small-group instruction is crucial for helping them develop deeper meanings of words and their relation to knowledge networks, building on the work in the whole-group setting. It provides a key opportunity for the children to practice their new words with guidance along the way. The frequent interactions allow you to make instant adjustments in children's understanding, helping them to develop a more thorough understanding of words and the concepts to which they are related. It is a more intensive instructional context for learning than the whole-group setting, which adds to its unique influence in promoting key opportunities to practice what children are learning in a safe, noncompetitive context.

Individual Work or Independent Time

In the early years, we often call this option *choice time*, or in the primary grades, *independent work time*. Regardless of its particular title, however, the focus is the same: to provide students with opportunities to engage in independent work that most intrigues them and that continues to build on what they have learned throughout the day. It is a time when children are encouraged to follow their interests and make choices among activities, giving them the responsibility for their own learning. Children can enjoy working alone or in small groups of their choosing, challenging each other as they share expertise, use richer vocabulary, and incorporate ideas of greater depth than in other settings.

Individual work time involves creating a strategic set of choices that help children take what they have learned and make it their own. It builds on the work you have done in small groups, and gives children opportunities to practice applying vocabulary words in new contexts. It is not time for worksheets or workbooks, but for active engagement in activities that consolidate children's thinking around a topic.

Here are some of things to consider about independent work time. First, it should involve students in authentic activity. It should support students' desire to explore, discuss, and meaningfully connect concepts and relationships that are relevant to their world—for example, taking notes on the progress of a science experiment and discussing how it is working is an authentic activity. Second, as you'll see in the following examples, we try to support activities that encourage application rather than a reiteration of what children have learned in the whole-group and small-group settings. In other words, independent activities are designed to *extend* what children have already learned by applying these words and concepts in a different context. In the course of these

IN THE CLASSROOM:
ENCOURAGING CHILDREN'S EXPLORATION

The children in Ms. Maribeth's prekindergarten classroom have been learning about the differences between living and nonliving things. Lilah and Elijah have been working at the science exploration center, organizing the items into two piles, living and nonliving. Soon, Lilah had a new idea for applying this concept, and Ms. Maribeth encouraged her continued exploration:

Lilah: Ms. Maribeth, I got an idea, but I don't know what to use to do it.

Ms. Maribeth: Why don't you share your idea and maybe I can think of a way to help?

Lilah: Well, me and Elijah, we want to put labels or some way of showing on the things all over the classroom to say if they're living or nonliving.

Elijah: But we need something to make the labels so they can stick on and stay there.

Ms. Maribeth: What an interesting idea. Could you use some sticky notes? Those are the little square papers that are sticky on the back. I have some in my supply drawer.

Lilah: Yeah. Maybe one color could be for living and a different color is for nonliving?

Ms. Maribeth: I think I have yellow and pink. Would that work?

Lilah: Yeah.

Elijah: Yeah.

Ms. Maribeth: I'll get them right now. This sounds like a great idea. Maybe when you're done you can tell the whole class about your exciting work.

investigations, although they will be reviewing what they have learned, they will be developing a deeper meaning of these ideas by examining them in multiple situations. And third, we always leave the door open for children to come up with new ideas for further exploration of their own.

Unlike small-group instruction, we do not assign children to independent activities, or require them to rotate to different tasks. Rather, we give them opportunities to make choices among a set of activities, and give them sufficient time to explore these ideas in depth. Time is an important feature here, as children will need to think through problems, use their developing inquiry skills to make predictions and discoveries, and work toward unique solutions depending on the particular tasks and activities.

During independent practice and work time, the teacher's role is to step back and let children try things on their own. They will need the time to practice and use their new learning in the context of authentic activities. This is where children need to make their own decisions about when, how, and what to learn, using the concepts that they have been practicing with guidance, but now on their own. In this process, you will then want to be an active observer of these activities, stepping in when necessary but stepping back out to encourage children to work out solutions with their peers and on their own.

It is also the time for you to informally assess how children are expressing their ideas in one-to-one conversations, how they go about a task, and their ability to interact with others, take turns speaking, and continue a conversation with you and others through multiple exchanges. These data can give you valuable information that you can use for additional instruction in small groups if necessary. By providing children with explicit information on words and concepts in a whole-group setting, followed by guided practice in small-group

instruction, and then lots of time and opportunity for review of these concepts in independent work settings that require application, you will help them to develop rich and robust understandings of words and the knowledge networks that surround them.

STRATEGIES FOR PROMOTING ONE-ON-ONE CONVERSATIONS WITH CHILDREN

You can learn a lot about children's knowledge of words and concepts, as well as their misconceptions, simply by talking to them. A key goal in the Common Core Standards is for children to participate in extended conversations where they take multiple turns in speaking. Here are some conversation starters and prompts that support extended conversations with children:

• Tell me about what you're working on. . .
• Tell me about what you are learning here. . .
• Tell me about what you are making/building/drawing/writing. . .
• Tell me about what you are pretending. . .

Prompts to extend a conversation:

- Tell me more. . .
- Why did you decide to work on that today?
- Why does that interest you?
- Tell me about what you're planning to do next. . .
- What do you predict will happen? Or, what do you think will happen next?
- Tell me what you think about. . .
- I'm wondering how your work relates to/is the same as/is different from [a concept the class is discussing]?
- What do you think would happen if you did [something slightly different]?

THINK ABOUT IT:
HOW ARE YOU USING WHOLE-GROUP TIMES?

Think about the ways you are currently using whole-group learning times. Are these times meeting learning goals for children? Ask yourself the following questions:

- Are most children attentive during whole-group times?
- Am I spending more time on discipline (e.g., "sit up," "raise your hand," "listen politely") or on actual teaching and learning?
- Are whole-group times fast paced and engaging?
- Are whole-group times going on too long for children?
- Do all children have an opportunity to participate?
- What am I doing to hold children's attention?
- Are children learning something new, or are they repeating the same routines and activities that they have done all year?

What we think about it:

In our work with teachers, we have found that whole-group times are often very long and filled with rote routines that do not build new knowledge or vocabulary for children. We have found that young children learn most during whole-group times when these times are brief, fast paced, engaging, and bursting with learning opportunities. Children are naturally more attentive when they listen to a wonderful book and when they are taught new and exciting words and ideas.

CREATING A COMPREHENSIVE VOCABULARY PROGRAM

In this section, we return to the classroom to demonstrate how teachers work to organize their content-rich vocabulary instruction. Our goal is to show how all the pieces work together, creating a comprehensive program that supports children's learning and retention of vocabulary, concepts, and comprehension. At the same time, we recognize that children's dispositions for learning—their curiosity, initiative, and engagement—are also critically important in the learning process. Therefore, you'll find a structure of activities that is designed to actively engage children's interests to promote their natural proclivity to learn about their world.

Starting with Whole-Group Instruction

The whole-group instructional time is dominated by our instructional regime using text sets as we have described extensively in Chapter 4. In this section, we focus on the ways in which a teacher may support children's learning and the types of responses we encourage during whole-group time. As an example, see the following planning sheet that Molly used for her topic of insects:

MOLLY'S PLANNING SHEET FOR INSECTS

Instructional Goals

- Children will learn key concepts and vocabulary for insects.
- Children will learn about life cycles and habitats.

Group Setting	Plan for Instruction
Whole Group	1. Review key concepts about insects [see Appendix A for a list of concepts]. 2. Read predictable books on insects (introduce word meanings). 3. Provide explicit explanation and picture cards for: ant, insect, life cycle, larva, segments, pupa (teach word meanings). 4. Use choral response and call and response for children to practice new words (children practice word meanings and concepts).

Small Group	1. *Discussion*: What makes an insect an insect (children practice new words) 2. Review meaning of *habitat* (review) 3. *Matching game*: Match insect to habitat (review)
Independent Work	1. Insect Sorting Bin [see box, "Strategies for Promoting One-on-One Conversations with Children"]: Children sort insects and non-insects (children apply words and concepts). 2. Use Insect Sorting Bin for ongoing progress monitoring: (1) Watch to see if children are sorting correctly. (2) Ask children *why* they are sorting insects the way they are and listen for key concepts and vocabulary (ongoing progress monitoring).

Molly's 1st-grade class is busy learning about the topic of insects and the big ideas that are common among these living things. She has created a text set (see Appendix A) that includes the vocabulary, concepts, and comprehension of information that reflect these big ideas, integrating both the Common Core Standards and science standards targeted to grade-level expectations. In this whole-group setting, her focus is to introduce the vocabulary and concepts and to build meaning, in effort to provide all students will a level playing field of information about the topic.

Molly will use two primary response patterns—choral responding and call and response—to support children's active engagement, and to ensure a well-paced whole-group lesson (with minimal management issues). Both are fairly straightforward techniques; however, most teachers find that they'll need some practice to fine-tune their activities to foster deeper, more authentic connections with students. We'll briefly review them here, and give you examples from Molly's classroom.

Choral Responding. This is a teaching technique that has been around forever, since the days of the one-room schoolhouse. It encourages all students to respond aloud and in unison to a teacher-directed question. Studies have shown a strong relationship between the frequency of student response during instruction and improved outcomes (Kegal, Bus, & IJzendoorn, 2011). This probably is due to the fact that it gives many opportunities for all students to actively participate, and provides you with immediate feedback on whether or not students understand what they are hearing so that you can instantly correct misconceptions. We find that it is especially useful for children who are English language learners, as it is more inclusive than many other techniques and allows them to become a part of the classroom team, without putting them on the spot. Finally, you will find that off-task behaviors and disruptive behaviors are significantly reduced when all children are encouraged to respond at the same time.

Here's what choral responding looks like in Molly's classroom. Molly is reading a patterned book, the first in her text set on insects. The book is designed to introduce children to some of the key words about insects:

Antonio the ant	Antonio has a life cycle
Antonio the ant	Antonio has a life cycle
6 segments	Egg—larva
3 legs	Pupa—adult
Antonio the ant	Antonio has a life cycle

Molly introduces children to the vocabulary, pointing to the pictures as she reads aloud. She gives a brief definition of the words, using the illustrations to give them more meaning. Then she reads the book again, this time stopping at the end of each page to engage children in saying the words along with her. For example, she'll read the last line on each page, stopping before the end of the sentence, "Antonio has a... , " waiting for the children to say the words "life cycle." The predictable pattern helps children to anticipate what will come next. When she reads the book again the next day, children will increasingly engage in the choral responding and reading.

Further, throughout this topic, she will introduce words using choral responses, stretching the sounds of the words and in some cases clapping them out. Together, the children all say and clap the words together—*me-ta-mor-pho-sus, cam-ou-flage, ha-bi-tat*—using the clapping to create a sense of the rhythm of each word. The choral responses help those children who might be having difficulty hearing the sounds in words or might need a bit more scaffolding from the group. This technique, then, provide a low-stress, fun way to learn a new skill.

Choral responses are a wonderful way to engage all children in rhymes and rhythms that are designed to be shared as a group. We often call them "tuning-in" responses based on Don Holdaway's work (1979), as they help to set the stage for all of us to come together as a community.

Call and Response. This is a music concept that is taught as early as preschool, with more in-depth variations emphasized all the way through 2nd grade. Call and response is a quickly paced question-and-answer technique that allows you to provide lots of interaction and reinforcement in an energetic and fun way. It is not echoing, because echoing is more like a choral response. Rather, this is listening to the "call" from the first person, processing it, and then providing a "response" that resolves the first call. Here's what it looks like:

Molly: Everybody look at me. What kind of insect did we see? Say it with me. [Cue children.]
Children and Teacher: Katydids.
Molly: Yes, the book was about katydids. Like most insects, katydids live outside. Because katydids are insects, they have six legs. Let's talk a little about katydids. Listen to the questions, and respond when I give the cue.
Teacher: Does a katydid live with people? Is a katydid a pet? [Cue children.]
Children: No.
Molly: Where does a katydid live? [Cue children.]
Children: Outside.
Molly: And what do insects use to smell?
Children: Antennae.

It's like a running dialogue or conversation between the teacher and the class as a unit. Because the whole group responds at the same time, you might say it's like getting 30 to 35 at-bats in a row. You will increase the frequency of children's responses dramatically using this technique. Plus, the children love the energetic pace, as you build on their previous responses.

Like all techniques, however, there are some things to consider when using call and response:

- **Keep it short.** Children should feel like they've been in an exercise class. Short practices energize; long practices get tedious.
- **Prepare ahead of time.** Keep your questions short and require one- to five-word answers. Longer answers can become convoluted and distorted.
- **Model before you get going.** We use simple hand motions to indicate when it's our time to speak and when it is time for the class to answer. It should be crisp when each party takes its appropriate turn.

- **Provide quick corrective feedback.** When necessary, provide feedback immediately.
- **Maintain an energetic pace.** Be prepared to ask the next question immediately after the response (or feedback). Fast pacing promotes students' participation and accuracy, and decreases off-task behavior.

For Molly, these two techniques have been her primary strategies for supporting interaction in whole-group instruction. Initially, however, she found them a bit intimidating and off-putting. For one, these types of quick responses were in contrast to her existing practice. Previously, she was used to having children raise their hands and calling on individual children, while helping others develop their "listening skills." Second, she was concerned that children were merely repeating and reciting rather than engaging in open-ended responses. Third, as an early childhood teacher, she was uncomfortable with the faster pacing.

What Molly came to recognize, however, is that children enjoyed the interaction; as she picked up pace, so did they. Furthermore, she found that the whole-group responses were a great lead-in for the slower, more open-ended small-group activities that followed whole group. She has also found that these techniques allow her to do more real teaching than behavior management, providing more instructional time for the children.

Small Group

Molly organizes small-group instruction by planning ahead in two ways. First, she intentionally forms heterogeneous groups so that children can support each other's learning; these children will stay together for the entire topic study. Second, she creates a schedule for rotating children in and out of small groups. Given many other competing activities, it may not be possible to have each involved in a small group every day. However, if a small-group time of 15 to 20 minutes is built into the schedule each day, each child can have a chance to be in a small group throughout a week. Molly keeps a list of who has been in a small group and who needs to be involved.

Today, children are building on the vocabulary taught in the whole-group lesson, learning more about what properties of insects make them living things. Molly wants the students to study some examples of insects and explore why there are so many different types. She also wants to keep a focus on the specific vocabulary words just introduced in the lesson: abdomen, antennae, larva, pupa, and thorax. She begins the lesson by asking the children, "What makes an insect an insect?" They review the basic properties. She then says, "Even though insects have the same common body parts, they are adapted to live in very different habitats with the ability to eat a variety of things. Let's play a match game and try to match which habitat goes with each insect, and talk about how the body parts are adapted to live in these different habitats."

Notice how Molly challenges the students to go beyond what was discussed in the whole-group lesson. Given its challenge, she stays with the group and does not circulate around the room to others, at least until the children have gotten a consolidated period of time and are clearly engaged and able to attend to the activity. In some cases, you can use self-correction techniques (such as answers on the back of the cards) that can allow students to complete activities on their own with minimal guidance.

Subsequent small-group activities can add challenge to the task. For example, Molly has her aide take one group outside to see what insects they can discover in their schoolyard. They use clear plastic containers, such as Tupperware, to catch and observe the insects with magnifying glasses. They write down their observations in their science notebooks, making sure that they release the insects where they were found. The children then compare the similarities and differences between the insects they found, and how each of the segments, although always present, are slightly different. In each of these activities, children are using their new vocabulary to add to their knowledge, creating a network of words, concepts, and information about these amazing creatures.

Finally, to support their ongoing interest in their investigations about insects, the teacher facilitates the children's interest in creating their own individual ant farms. Using a small, clear plastic cup, each student gathers some dirt with live ants. They scoop up enough dirt to fill their individual cups halfway, add a little water to make the dirt damp, and put on a top to make sure that the ants don't escape. They feed the ants one bird seed, one leaf piece, or one wet sugared crumb every few days, along with adding five or six water drops. After the ants start digging, if the children look carefully they can see the tunnels and what the ants are doing and how they dig. From this vantage point, they can get an ant's-eye view, and better understand how ants live. All of these observations are carefully recorded in their science notebooks.

Notice that in the small-group activities, the explicit instruction in vocabulary and concepts of the whole-group context gives way to a greater emphasis on vocabulary instruction in use. Set in meaningful contexts, children now have reasons to participate in collaborative conversations and use their vocabulary for descriptive purposes. In a content-rich setting, they now have something to talk about, and are developing the academic language that will be essential for them to eventually become college- and career-ready.

Independent Work Time

One of the challenges of working in small groups is what to do with the remaining students in the classroom who also need to be involved in productive work. This is where careful planning and effective use of other resources are essential. To support the content-rich focus of vocabulary instruction, we create discovery centers, small areas within the classroom where students can work alone or together on independent (no teacher direct involvement) content-rich activities. Discovery centers are designed to encourage students to try out investigations that are tied to the topic area on their own or with their peers.

These centers use literacy skills but they are not about literacy. Rather, a discovery center is a space where students can practice what they are learning, explore topics through greater research and observation. A discovery center should be a "go-to" place. Think about the types of materials or objects you can include so that your students can engage in a variety of self-directed exploration activities that provide opportunities for extending and elaborating on the activities in the small- and whole-group settings. We also try to include materials and activities that further develop children's reasoning and inquiry skills through observing, comparing, classifying, and measuring objects.

We try to choose content, materials, objects, events, and experiences that help build and elaborate on students understanding of key concepts. These are the things we consider:

- A discovery center should be in a designated area, and should be carefully labeled.
- Include student-world and student-friendly materials.
- Location, location, location! The center should be accessible, within reach, at eye level, and ready for discovery.
- It's important to keep the center interesting by adding new materials and rotating others out when the focus is on a new topic.

Regardless of the topic, certain categories of materials are always included in discovery centers:

Basic tools: thermometer, measuring cups and spoons, test tubes, rulers, balances and scales, magnifying lens, etc.

Concept-driven collections: Helping students make comparisons and contrasts, sorts, and matches is central for building their understanding of concepts and generalizations. For example, we include collections that encourage students to sort plastic insects (six legs) versus spiders (eight legs). You can also include multisensory discovery collections such as mystery boxes.

Kid finds: We encourage students to bring in their "finds" related to the topic they are studying in the discovery center.

Student- and teacher-created materials: Consider adding concept-driven posters, such as collages of insects or habitats, or other themes.

In addition, we like to include a "Question of the Week" poster, such as "What do insects do in the winter?" Or try a "Hypothesis" poster, which raises a question for the students to explore, such as "Why does the caterpillar build a cocoon?" In addition, you'll see that we like to include additional manipulative materials for hands-on learning (see the In the Classroom feature).

The discovery center should offer lots of choices within the parameters of your topic focus, with all options geared to be self-directed so that children can work independently or with several other children. When carefully planned, having some students engaged in the discovery center will provide time for you to check in with individual children, as well as spend concentrated time with your small groups. The activities in the discovery center will allow children to review vocabulary and concepts and build background knowledge on their own terms. As a result, we find that the time devoted for independent practice is time well spent.

IN THE CLASSROOM: EXAMPLES OF DISCOVERY CENTERS

We use discovery centers as places where children can explore a topic further during independent work time. The teacher sets up these spaces, but all of the necessary materials are available so that children can work and explore independently. Discovery centers work well for choice times in early childhood classrooms and for independent work times or centers in elementary school classrooms. Here are descriptions of three discovery centers from a class that was studying insects, and three from a class that was studying plants:

Discovery Centers for Insects

Insect Sorting

Materials: insect/non-insect plastic figurines
Exploration: Children can sort the bugs by identifying which are insects and which are not insects (sand table can be used for this activity).

Insect Terrarium or Ant Farm

Materials: ant farm and/or glass container with real insects (such as feeder crickets), magnifying glass, paper, pencils, markers
Exploration: Children can explore real insects at work. Children can draw and write about their observations.

Insect Life-Cycle Sequence

Materials: laminated pictures showing each stage of the butterfly life cycle
Exploration: Children can put the stages of the butterfly life cycle in
    sequential order. Children can tell a friend about the life cycle of a
    butterfly.

Discovery Centers for Plants

Seed Exploration

Materials: a variety of seeds, magnifying glasses, tweezers
Exploration: Children can investigate different types of plant seeds and
    sort them according to different characteristics (e.g., color, size).

Planting

Materials: bean seeds for planting, topsoil, cups, spoons, watering
    container, cotton balls, grass seed, plastic wrap, rubber bands
Exploration: Children can plant two different types of seeds—bean seeds in
    soil and grass seed on soaked cotton balls. They will need to cover them
    with plastic wrap and put them in a sunny location to watch them grow.

Dramatic Play: Gardener/Farmer

Materials: child-size garden tools, a variety of artificial plants and flowers,
    gardening gloves, watering can
Exploration: Children can pretend they are gardeners or farmers.

THINK ABOUT IT:
PLANNING FOR LEARNING ACROSS GROUPING
STRUCTURES

Try using this sheet as you plan your vocabulary instruction. As you plan,
think about which settings might be best for specific learning goals for children. Also think about our instructional framework. Consider which settings
work best for teaching new words and concepts, for providing opportunities
for children to practice and review, and also for ongoing progress monitoring.

Instructional Goals

-
-

(Continued)

Group Setting	Plan for Instruction
Whole Group	1. 2. 3.
Small Group	1. 2. 3.
Independent Work	1. 2. 3.

What we think about it:

Because vocabulary instruction needs to take place throughout the day, teachers need to plan carefully to make sure that this critical instruction does not get neglected. Teachers not only need to consider which words will be taught, but also *how* and *when* they will be taught. Children need multiple encounters with the same words and concepts to solidify their knowledge. Careful attention to planning and organization ensures that all children in your classroom will have the opportunity to learn the words and concepts that they need for school.

CONCLUSIONS

In some critical ways, vocabulary development is unique among all the skills we teach in the early years. It cannot be consigned to a particular time of day. Neither can it be taught only through teachable moments or through the normal daily discourse between teachers and children and children with their peers. Throughout this chapter, we have emphasized how the organizational design of your classroom can support a more comprehensive approach to vocabulary instruction. Quality whole-group instruction is imperative for word learning, as it helps set the stage for instructional activities in the classroom and provides a shared vocabulary and language that helps to engage all your learners. Small-group instruction is enormously beneficial because it affords the opportunity for you to devote attention to children, and this, in turn, has important implications for children's cognitive development as well as their social and emotional development. Independent work time builds on children's desire to create, to invent new solutions, to strive to learn more, and to build their own interpretations of how their world works. In this respect, it not only engages their minds, but their very initiative to learn.

6 How Do We Know Children Are Learning?

Most of us can sense when children seem to be progressing in learning. We can see it in their active engagement in tasks. It might relate to their initiative in answering and asking questions. Or it might be noticed in their eagerness to participate in lessons. It might also be reflected in their uses of language, or their ability to apply what they've learned to new activities. Together, these types of behaviors may give us a good indication that children are acquiring the skills they will need to become successful learners.

In the age of Common Core standards, however, these indications will not be enough. Increasingly, teachers will need to provide concrete evidence that children—even starting at the preschool level—are learning and are on target to meet these rigorous standards. You will need to record and document children's progress in ways that effectively convey what they are learning and how they are consistent with grade-specific expectations. And you will want to be confident that the gains you are seeing are both reliable and valid—and represent true indicators that children are on a trajectory of success.

In this chapter, we'll first describe several issues to consider in assessing vocabulary. We'll provide a number of techniques to use to reliably measure children's progress in learning content-rich vocabulary as well as concept development. We'll then show you how these measures can successfully describe children's progress, providing a convincing case for meeting the rigorous standards in the Common Core. Finally, we'll sum up, giving you a set of principles that highlight the essential features of our approach.

ASSESSING VOCABULARY DEVELOPMENT

It's not easy to assess vocabulary growth and development. Although early on we can track children's vocabulary acquisition with some degree of consistency using parent reports, once children get beyond

3 years of age, their language will grow increasingly idiosyncratic, based on the types of day-to-day experiences they may have as well as their relationships with caregivers. Therefore, there is no set corpus of typical words that children are likely to have, and that we can expect them to know. Unlike alphabet knowledge, where there is a finite number of letters to learn, vocabulary is an unconstrained skill, one in which all of us continue to learn throughout our lifetimes.

Consequently, standardized assessments (e.g., Peabody Picture Vocabulary Tests) are particularly problematic in measuring vocabulary growth. Generally, these measures rely on test developers selecting words by their perceived difficulty level. Ultimately, scores on such tests derive their meaning from making comparisons between children, not words, at large, which is why we call them norm-referenced tests. Under such circumstances, all we know is that a given student performed better, or worse, than the average student on the set of words that happened to be on the test. We know nothing about what the scores say about students' knowledge of any identifiable domain or corpus of words. Further, these tests place a great deal of emphasis on children's prior-knowledge meaning that they are not particularly sensitive to instructional intervention (Pearson, Hiebert, & Kamil, 2007). This means that the hard work you do in vocabulary instruction will often not be well recorded due to the qualities of the test, and not the quality of your instruction.

It is for these reasons, among others (e.g., developmental appropriateness; Neuman, Copple, & Bredekamp, 2000), that we use evaluative techniques that are designed to measure the effects of our teaching. Specifically, effective assessment strategies make it possible for teachers to:

- monitor and document children's specific progress on standards over time
- ensure that instruction is responsive and appropriately matched to what children are and are not able to do
- customize instruction to meet individual children's strengths and needs
- enable children to recognize their own growth and development
- identify children who might benefit from more intensive levels of instruction

From our perspective, teaching and assessment are complementary processes; one activity informs the other. Quality assessment therefore should be designed to identify children's strengths and needs and monitor their progress toward specific learning goals. It should inform program planning and decision making to ensure that classroom instruction is responsive to and appropriate for children's current levels, and certainly should not be used for high-stakes purposes.

ASSESSMENT ACTIVITIES

Most important, assessment techniques should measure what we teach. Otherwise, we are giving unfair advantage to those children who may come from more economically advantaged communities than others. In this section, we describe a number of assessment formats that can be adapted for use in your program. Notice several key features of these assessments. For one, each focuses on *one* particular aspect of vocabulary. In other words, one measure doesn't try to do too much. Second, we tend to use game-like formats. Children are likely to score more optimally when the task involves more active responses. Third, we try to use different formats to account for children's linguistic diversity and diverse backgrounds. For example, many of our English language learners will demonstrate remarkable progress in vocabulary when they are given a receptive measure (e.g., one that involves pointing to a picture) as opposed to an expressive task, which might require the children to provide a word label. And fourth, you'll see that we try to keep things relatively simple so that teachers can score the assessments quickly to get results.

The following assessments are designed to give you examples of how we measure children's progress. They are certainly not end-all or be-all measures. In other words, you will want to continue documenting children's learning through portfolios (see accompanying box), which provide vivid examples of their activities, and anecdotal notes, which can say so much about children's interests and eagerness to learn. Further, you won't necessarily want to use all of the assessment tasks. Rather, these examples provide a number of formats for you to consider in your program.

CREATING A PORTFOLIO

A portfolio is a wonderful way to track and document children's work. A student portfolio is a systematic collection of student work and related materials that reflect his or her interests, activities, accomplishments, and achievements. The collection should be more than just a folder of a child's work. Rather, it should show some evidence of reflection, self-evaluation, and specific guidelines for the quality of the work and the selection of content. Your goal is to help students assemble portfolios that illustrate their talents, interests, and capabilities, and tell their stories of special achievement.

Items for Portfolios

- Evidence of interests, special activities
- Checklists of progress
- Examples of a child's writing, drawing, and/or unique creation
- Documents
- Anecdotes and special notes
- Informal assessments of progress
- Running records
- Story retellings

Advantages of Portfolios

- Allow children's performance to be measured based on genuine samples of work
- Provide different ways to examine how a child might be learning or demonstrating a particular learning style
- Provide opportunities for rich conversations with parents
- Allow achievement goals to be seen from multiple perspectives reflecting multiple dimensions

We measure children's learning starting with the vocabulary words that we have taught. We don't stop there, however. Increasingly, our tasks involve the measurement of concepts that underlie these words and the "big ideas"—the content-rich knowledge that we're hoping children have learned throughout our program. As we go along, you'll also see greater attention to the application of these concepts to new words in new contexts, and greater attention to expressive language. Keeping in mind the increasing number of English language learners in our classrooms, we generally start with receptive measures (in which children can respond by pointing, indicating that they have listening comprehension) and move toward expressive measures (in which they can express their understanding using the words that they have learned).

The examples that follow come from our topic on insects. Note the progression of tasks, how they begin to dig deeper into depth of knowledge beyond the mere labeling of words.

Measuring Growth in Children's Vocabulary

We begin with a basic vocabulary task that asks children to identify the new word that we have taught. We show children a card with three pictures (Figure 6.1), and ask them to point to the picture of the target word. Notice that we try to make it a bit challenging by including some logical distractors. In this case, one of the distractors is another bug—from the same category of insects—and the other is related to the theme of insects but does not fall into the category. We mix up the cards for each child so that the order is changed, and include about ten of these cards to get an overall assessment of whether each child has learned the words that we've taught over the 2-week topic study. This assessment takes about 2 minutes per child, and we do it on a one-to-one basis.

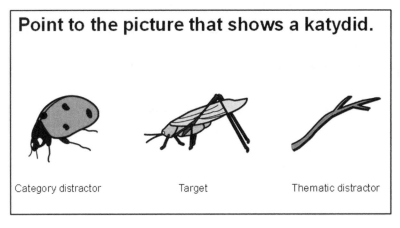

Figure 6.1: Ability to Identify Words

This is a receptive vocabulary task to measure children's ability to identify target vocabulary. In this task, three pictures are presented on each page and the child is asked to point to the picture representing the target word. Of the three pictures, one is the target, one is a distractor that is thematically related to the target, and the other is a distractor that is categorically related to the target.

Measuring Children's Concept Knowledge

Over the years, we have found a number of ways to tap children's conceptual knowledge with reliability and validity. Here's one task that is easy to put together and helps you to understand children's reasoning. It involves asking children a simple yes-or-no question, followed by asking them to justify their answers (Figure 6.2). It works like this:

Teacher: Is a ladybug an insect?
Child: Yes. (or no)
Teacher: Why? (or why not)

Similar to our previous measure, this concept assessment examines children's understanding of category membership and conceptual properties. However, in this task, children will be asked a series of simple yes-or-no questions about the properties of a target word and whether a target word belongs in a particular category—for example: "Is a ladybug an insect?" and "Does a ladybug have three body parts?" Children are then asked to explain their response (e.g., "Why do you think a ladybug is/is not an insect?"). Based on our experiences, this

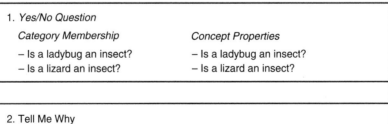

Figure 6.2: A Concept Measure

assessment is a bit harder for children than the previous concept task because it relies on expressive language.

The assessment allows you to see whether children understand that different words may come under the same conceptual umbrella. You can score the assessment by the total number of correct responses, or you can examine children's reasoning to see whether they are simply guessing or not. You'll notice that the first part of the assessment may be easy for your English language learners to respond to, but the second part is more difficult because it involves expressive language. Therefore, we've adapted this task in several ways to take into account children's developing language skills. In other words, we want this task to be about tapping children's conceptual knowledge, and not confounding it with their "language ability."

Here's a task that allows you to measure the same type of conceptual knowledge without the heavy emphasis on expressive vocabulary. Once again, we use pictures (Figure 6.3), and ask the child to point to the picture that indicates his or her knowledge of how the word relates to the larger concept. In this case, we will not ask for a justification; rather, the task only examines the child's ability to identify how a word is connected to a concept. For both tasks, we include about 10 to 12 items, and it takes approximately 5 minutes to administer, even when we ask for explanations.

This is also a receptive vocabulary task that specifically measures a child's understanding of a target word's category membership and of

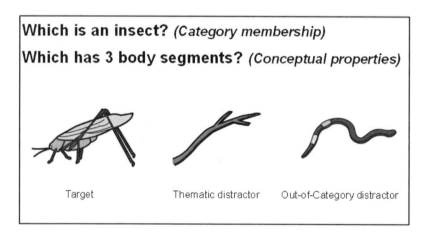

Figure 6.3: A Concept Assessment

the conceptual properties related to a category. For this task, a child is shown three pictures, a target picture (e.g., a katydid), a picture thematically related to the target (e.g., a twig), and an out-of-category distractor (e.g., a worm). The child is then asked either to identify which picture belongs to a particular category ("Which is an insect?") or to identify the picture that possesses a particular category attribute (e.g., "Which has three body segments?).

Now here's yet another measure we've developed to measure children's conceptual knowledge, and this one is a bit fun for children to do. It's called the Picky Peter task (Figure 6.4), and we've used it with a number of different topics. Further developed by Julie Dwyer in our group (Neuman, Newman, & Dwyer, 2011), it involves using a puppet named Peter along with two large bins that are placed on the table next to the child. To introduce the task, we say:

> Today we are going to play a game with my friend named "Picky Peter."
> Peter is picky because he only likes [TOPIC, e.g., in this case "insects"].
> You are going to help Picky Peter by sorting through these pictures. The
> things that are insects will go in Picky Peter's bin and the things that
> aren't will go in the other bin.

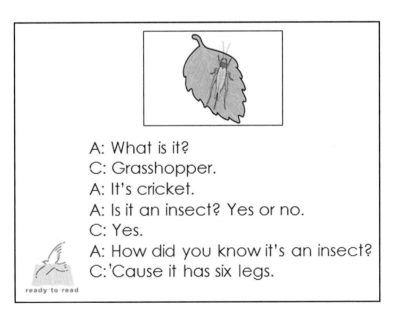

A: What is it?
C: Grasshopper.
A: It's cricket.
A: Is it an insect? Yes or no.
C: Yes.
A: How did you know it's an insect?
C:'Cause it has six legs.

ready·to·read

Figure 6.4: Picky Peter Task

We then show a picture and ask "What is this?" After the child either responds or is given the correct answer, we ask the child to put the picture in one bin or the other. After the child makes his or her choice about the picture and whether it is or is not an insect, we ask the child to justify his or her response.

Our Picky Peter task is a type of word-sort that involves children in putting words into categories and then asking them for their justification or evidence as to why they responded that way. It is a beginning strategy that may help teach children how to form an argument, a critical topic in the Common Core Standards. Children enjoy the task because it allows them to respond at their comfort level. For example, some children will be at a point where they can articulate their rationale. This gives us a good sense of how they are organizing their new knowledge and the degree to which they're developing a rudimentary sense of category, which is essential for concept development. At the same time, some children will sort the pictures correctly, but when asked for their reasoning they may simply say "'cause," not being quite yet able to provide an argument or rational evidence for their choice. This is all very useful information for understanding where students are in the course of developing basic argumentation and evidence as outlined in the Common Core Standards.

Big Ideas

Big ideas are concepts that facilitate the most efficient and broadest acquisition of knowledge across a range of topics within a domain. Essentially, they reflect the content knowledge that children have acquired throughout the work on a topic. In this respect, big ideas reflect both the academic terms (e.g., word knowledge) and the network of concepts (e.g., world knowledge) that form the very basic foundation for later learning.

We like to use a game-like structure for this kind of task. Here we are interested in children's understanding of the life cycle of an insect, which is one of the big ideas that is related to our topic. In this example (Figure 6.5), the child is first shown a picture of an insect at one point in its life cycle. Then, we show him or her two pictures at two other points in the insect's life cycle. The child is then asked to identify which of the two pictures presents the *next* point in the life cycle. For example, a child is shown a picture of a chrysalis, followed by pictures of a butterfly and a caterpillar, and is then asked, "When this

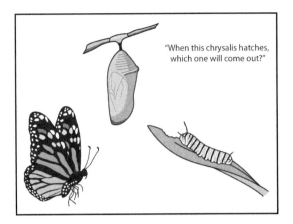

"When this chrysalis hatches, which one will come out?"

Figure 6.5: Assessing Big Ideas

chrysalis hatches, which will come out?" If he or she understands different points in an insect's life cycle, there is some indication that the big ideas have been understood. We usually include about six items, giving us a good set of big ideas from which to tap.

This is the first of two types of measures that examine children's ability to identify "big ideas." In this case, we are examining children's understanding of "life cycles." In this task, children are shown a picture of an insect at one point in its life cycle. They are then shown two pictures of the insect at two other points in the life cycle. Children are asked to identify which of the two pictures presents the next point (or the previous point) in the life cycle. For example, children may be shown a picture of a chrysalis, and then shown a picture of a butterfly and a caterpillar. They are next asked, "When this chrysalis hatches, which will come out?" If children have an understanding of the different life cycles, they should be able to make the correct choice.

Here's another example, using a somewhat different task. In this case, the big idea is "protection" and how animals seek to protect themselves from predators (Figure 6.6). In this task, the child is shown two pictures, one showing a feature or behavior that could be used for protection, the other showing neither a feature nor a behavior. The child is then asked to identify which of the two pictures shows the insect "better protected from an enemy." For example, the child may be shown a picture of a moth on a rock and a moth on grass and asked which is better protected from predators. If the child has an understanding of different types of protection (in this case, camouflage), he or she is likely to make the right choice.

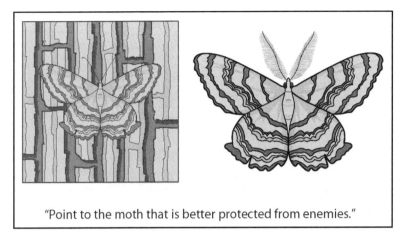

"Point to the moth that is better protected from enemies."

Figure 6.6: A "Big Ideas" Assessment Task

Here's a slightly different way to address children's understanding of big ideas. In this case, we are interested in children's knowledge of how an insect protects itself. In this task, children are shown two pictures of an insect, one showing a feature or behavior that could be used for protection, and the other not showing that feature or behavior. Children are then asked to identify which of the two pictures shows the insect "better protected from a predator (or an enemy)." For example, children may be shown a picture of a moth on a rock and a moth on grass and asked which is better protected from predators. If children have an understanding of different types of protection (in this case, camouflage), they should be able to make the right choice.

The Concepts of Comprehension Assessment (COCA; Billman et al., 2008) is a task aimed at measuring a child's ability to comprehend information books. In this task, the teacher reads aloud from an informational book, and on each page are questions to ask the child about what is going on and what may be learned from the book (Figure 6.7). For example, on one page a child may be read a sentence, and then be asked to point to the picture that best matches what was just read. On another page a child may be asked to recall what was learned from that page.

If you are interested in this assessment, we recommend that you contact the author at Michigan State University in East Lansing, Michigan or the co-author, Nell Duke (nkduke@umich.edu).

All together, these types of assessments are designed to give you a sense of how we determine children's progress. You'll see the heavy

Salmon lay their eggs at the bottom of streams

"Point to the picture that goes with the words I just read"

Figure 6.7: Concepts of Comprehension Assessment

use of picture prompts because our goal is to uncover children's developing word and world knowledge. Years ago, Bill Nagy came up with the important insight that vocabulary learning is incremental; often, we don't recognize the important but real gains in children's vocabulary knowledge unless we measure them carefully. Giving children a series of tasks like these that are informal and game-like allows you to better understand the developmental progression of their learning, and their progress toward achieving the rigorous standards of the Common Core.

EVIDENCE OF CHILDREN'S LEARNING

In the past 6 years, we have had opportunities to test our model of vocabulary learning in many different settings, and with children who come from low-income communities, many of whom are English language learners. Here, we'd like to highlight some of the things we've learned, and why it is so important to focus on content-rich instruction.

For those who are interested in more detail on the studies themselves, you'll find them in the References section.

In all, we have studied vocabulary learning with over 2,000 children. We've conducted design studies in an attempt to understand the active ingredients of quality instruction, as well as randomized controlled trials examining the impact of interventions. We've looked at vocabulary learning in the home and the school, and the environmental supports that are typical for young children. From these studies, we can summarize the following points:

- Children from low-socioeconomic circumstances are not receiving the type of language supports they will need to achieve the standards in the Common Core—in the home or in school. Children who have limited opportunities for academic language learning in the home most often go to schools with similar limited opportunities (Wright & Neuman, 2011).
- Early literacy instruction in many classrooms in low-income communities has been reduced to the basic skills of learning letters, sounds, and basic mathematics, with very limited time devoted to content instruction. With little time devoted to science and social studies, children will not develop the background skills needed for comprehending text.
- Despite calls for increasing the amount of informational text reading, little time is spent on it in classroom instruction.
- English language learners often go unnoticed and are not receiving the language supports early on in school that they will need to become successful.

Together, these findings suggest that children are likely to struggle to meet the rigorous Common Core Standards emphasizing the importance of the integration of knowledge and ideas in texts, the ability to make arguments based on evidence, and the ability to analyze similarities and differences among texts if we do not provide more targeted instruction in vocabulary in ways that help children build knowledge networks.

To better understand what needs to happen, let's focus on what children are capable of when given the opportunity to learn in content-rich settings. In a randomized controlled experiment (generally considered the "gold standard" of research), we examined how a year-long program of content-rich instruction might compare with classrooms using their typical day-to-day curriculum in 24 Head Start classrooms in a high-poverty urban area that was severely affected by the recent economic recession. Classrooms were evenly divided into treatment and control groups, with the treatment condition participating in a 12-minute, 4-day-per-week program of content-rich vocabulary instruction.

However, in addition to this traditional experimental design, we raised another question. We reasoned that it was not simply enough to compare two similar groups of students; rather, we needed to understand if content-rich instruction might "level the playing field" by helping low-income and language-minority children reach the same standards and skills that middle- and upper-income children have when they enter school. In other words, could quality vocabulary instruction early on improve the odds that children would come to school with the vocabulary and conceptual skills that are essential to ensure that they are ready to learn? To answer this question, we measured children's progress from two additional groups: a sample of middle-class children in a state-related preschool program and a sample of children from a university-based program, where over half of the children's parents were PhD students or faculty. In total, we measured more than 1,200 3- and 4-year-old children's progress in vocabulary and conceptual knowledge over a year's time. In addition, we then came back a half a year later to see if the gains were sustained.

Using both standardized measures and some of the assessments described earlier, Figure 6.8 begin to tell a compelling story. It shows what we began to see by the middle of the year.

As you can see in Figure 6.8, the gains for children in the treatment group were dramatic compared to those of the control group, which remained rather stable. More interesting, however, was that as the words got harder, the children did better, so that by the end of the year there was no statistical difference between the treatment children and the middle-class and upper-middle-class children.

Now let's take a look at children's conceptual development (see Figure 6.9). This is an area that is often not considered in the early years, yet it is central to children's developing comprehension. Here you'll note that the scores of the Head Start treatment group even exceeded those of the middle-class children by the middle of the year,

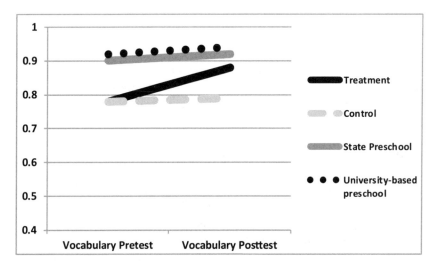

Figure 6.8: Vocabulary Progress of Children

and were statistically on par with the upper-class children at both the middle and the end of the year. In other words, these children were engaged in using similar abstract language skills and concepts that their more economically advantaged peers were using as these children were about to enter kindergarten.

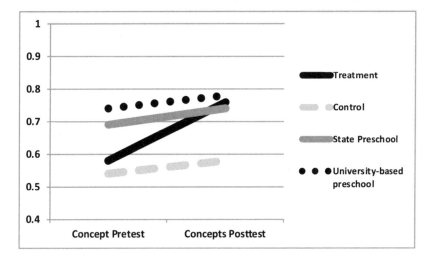

Figure 6.9: Children's Growth in Developing Concepts

Now, let's turn to our English language learners. When we looked at the differences between native English speakers and second language learners, we found some interesting and very relevant results. Our assessments indicated significant growth in vocabulary and conceptual knowledge for both native and second language learners (see Figure 6.10). However, for those in the control group, their understandings of conceptual categories throughout the year actually went *down*. These findings suggest that in settings where the language is not comprehensible and no effort is made to help these children learn concepts, second language learners' growth in concepts is stymied.

Finally, we were curious about transfer: whether children who develop conceptual knowledge in some topics can apply their understanding to an entirely new topic. In particular, we were interested in whether our content-rich instruction supported children's *self-learning*. In this extension task, children were introduced to six unfamiliar objects, half of which were tested with a category-related property (e.g., "Can you use a backhoe to make things?"); the remaining objects were tested using an unrelated property (e.g., "Can you use a backhoe to count?"). Children completed three steps for each of the six unfamiliar objects. First, they were asked to identify

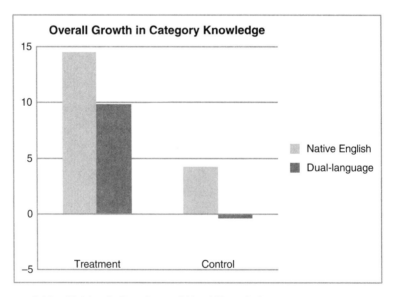

Figure 6.10: Children's Developing Word Knowledge

the target object from a set of three pictures; this step helped ensure that the object was, in fact, unfamiliar. Children were next told the name of the target object and its category membership (e.g., "This is a vise. It's a tool."). Third, children were asked whether the object possessed certain category properties (e.g., "Can you use a vise to make things?"). (See Figure 6.11).

We found that the children in our treatment group were significantly more able to make connections to concepts and to extend their learning to a topic that they were less familiar with. In other words, good-quality instruction, structured in a way that allows children to begin to make knowledge networks, helps them to think more conceptually. In this example, children were able to use their existing knowledge for self-teaching purposes. Children's conceptual knowledge appeared to bootstrap their ability to (1) determine the meaning of unfamiliar words and (2) figure out how these unfamiliar objects related to a larger category. Consequently, with this type of targeted instruction, these children not only made educationally meaningful gains, they closed the gap, achieving at levels consistent with those of more economically advantaged children. This suggests, quite simply, that we have just begun to tap these children's potential.

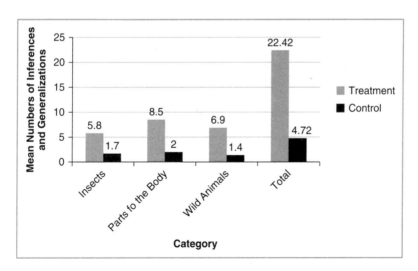

Figure 6.11: Children's Ability to Generalize Categorical Knowledge to New Words

REDUCING VOCABULARY DISPARITIES THROUGH HIGH-QUALITY INSTRUCTION

In this final section, we highlight some of the critical features emphasized throughout this book. We have argued that for children to be successful in the Age of Common Core Standards, they will need a rich and in-depth knowledge of words and concepts that will allow them to develop the comprehension skills so essential to learning throughout the grades. Our approach focuses on a set of principles, which we summarize here.

Principle 1: The Notion of Acceleration

Throughout this book we have argued that we need to accelerate children's vocabulary development. Hart and Risley's (2003) statistics of the differential in exposure—30 million words—prior to kindergarten between low- and middle-income children are not going to go away unless we aggressively put in place self-teaching strategies. This gap is not going to close easily, particularly when we consider that children have spent 20,000 hours with their parents prior to school entry, and the number of hours of instruction in a school year may represent as little as 540 hours. To narrow these statistics, it will not be enough to merely improve children's vocabulary. Rather, we have to accelerate its development—to create self-teaching strategies early on so that children can learn new words on their own.

Principle 2: Content-Rich Vocabulary

The reason that vocabulary is so critically important in learning is that it is children's entry to knowledge and the world of ideas. To talk about their ideas, whether about the weather, seasons, or holidays, children will need content-related words. In order to have a good conversation, for example, about visiting a museum or going to the apple orchard, children will need a threshold of content-specific words to talk about their ideas. Selecting content-rich words that represent labels of common items therefore is essential for building and ultimately activating background knowledge. For example, you can't have much of a conversation about planting in the spring without an understanding of such words as *stems, leaves,* and *bulbs,* as well as of the general concepts of what makes plants grow. And your conversation will be all that more interesting if you can talk about photosynthesis and the role of carbon dioxide and oxygen in plant life.

In addition, children will need what we describe as *supporting words*—words to talk about these concepts, as they serve the central function of helping to examine, contrast and compare, and differentiate phenomena. Right from the very beginning, we teach children words like *predict, observe, compare,* and *contrast* so that we may stretch their understanding of words in new ways. Further, we always give them *challenge words*—which make them feel like they are "grown up" learners. Rather than call someone a "weather reporter," for example, we use the word *meteorologist,* or *weather forecaster;* when we read a book, we talk about the *illustrator* and not someone who merely draws pictures. Children love to use words like these, and they become second-hand nature when they are part of the classroom instruction.

Principle 3: Organization of Word Knowledge

Throughout this book, we have recommended ways for you to help structure children's learning so that they can retain and access it more easily. Too often words are taught in isolation, with little attention to how these words may fit within larger concepts and ideas. Children learn them and then just as quickly forget them because they do not understand their relationships. Some of the lessons we have learned include the following:

- Children learn new vocabulary in the context of acquiring new knowledge; concepts come in clusters that are systematically interrelated.
- Children tend to organize information into meaningful categories that allow for better generalization and application to new contexts.
- Vocabulary knowledge becomes more efficient and supports children's self-learning as they become independent readers and writers.

Principle 4: The Use of Text Sets

Storybook narratives are a wonderful source for learning new words and developing children's imagination. However, informational books provide children with knowledge about their world that can be used to gain greater depth in content knowledge and facilitate comprehension. In our work, lessons are organized into related topics—such as insects, wild animals, animals that live in water—to prime children's background knowledge in high-utility content and strategically integrate concepts with previously learned material. What we have learned throughout our work is that children need scaffolding to utilize and enjoy informational books to their fullest extent. In developing text sets, we use many different genres of books to familiarize children with the words and concepts found in informational books. We find that combining predictable texts, storybooks, and informational books in text sets helps children identify with the concepts we're trying to teach and engages them in way that best promotes word and world knowledge.

Principle 5: Gradual Release of Control

This principle refers to the guidance, assistance, and support that you provide to your learners. Teachers use different degrees of support, or scaffolding, to assist their young learners at the initial stage, and then systematically and gradually release control so that children can try new activities on their own. In the beginning, for example, we focus on explicit explanations, helping children to "get set"—providing critical background information so that the children establish a purpose for learning. We then encourage work in small groups and independent activities to help "give meaning," to deepen their understanding of the topic. As the instructional regime progresses, it becomes more and more important to "build bridges" to what children have already learned and what they will learn. You'll increasingly release more control to the children, letting them take the lead. Finally, there are times, especially during independent activities, when it's appropriate for you to step back and let the children initiate activities. Because children now have better background and more words to discuss their ideas, conversations at this stage encourage children to elaborate on what they have learned and "give it a go."

Principle 6: The Importance of Practice and Distributed Review

Although vocabulary learning might seem like its natural, it's not. Children will need many different opportunities and examples to practice what they are learning. To get proficient at any skill, you need lots of practice. It's important, therefore, not to underestimate the time necessary for review and continual practice. The best way to facilitate review and practice is to have a coherent curriculum that builds on a progression of topics. In this way, children come in contact with similar words and concepts and have opportunities to build deeper meaning as they further develop their understandings.

Principle 7: Strategic Integration of Activities

Another theme that we've tried to promote is the importance of linking whole-group, small-group, and independent activities more strategically than in the past as a way to build children's knowledge. Think of every organizational design as providing you with a special opportunity. The whole-group setting provides a wonderful opportunity to develop shared information, a coming together of community to learn. Small-group activities enable you to dig deeper, to better tailor instruction to children's needs and to hear and engage them in richer interactions. Independent activities, ideally, allow children to use what they've learned and create self-learning opportunities that further their interests and desire to learn. The linkage between all of these activities builds a momentum in which ideas begin to take center stage.

Principle 8: Don't Be Afraid to Challenge Young Children

Repeatedly in our work we have been delightfully surprised by children's ability to stretch their thinking in ways that we would have never anticipated. Children love to become experts in various domains; they tend to be goal oriented and actively seek information. Words provide an important entryway. Classrooms in which children discover new words and become fascinated with the ideas they represent are those that prepare children to meet the challenges of learning in the age of the Common Core Standards.

The Common Core State Standards offer all of us a unique opportunity to challenge ourselves and to challenge our young students in learning all about words. Let's take advantage of this "moment in time" to engage children in the exciting world of content-rich learning. It is our belief that how well we do this will ultimately depend on whether reading and writing become meaningful parts of children's lives. This, in turn, will depend on the people who are most important to them—both outside and inside of school—and on the messages we convey to them about the "having of wonderful ideas" (Duckworth, 2006).

Examples of Text Sets

TOPIC: WEATHER

Concepts

- Weather conditions are constantly changing.
- There are weather patterns associated with each season.
- Various types of weather conditions are associated with temperature, precipitation, and wind conditions.
- There are tools to measure temperature, precipitation, and wind speed.
- Meteorologists use weather patterns to forecast weather.

Text Set

Predictable

Cotton, C., & Steptoe, J. (2008). *Rain play*. New York: Henry Holt and Co.

> A group of children are playing in the park when it starts to rain. They stay to enjoy some "running, romping, puddle-stomping" rainy-day fun.

Fiction

Koscielniak, B. (1995). *Geoffrey groundhog predicts the weather.* Boston: Houghton Mifflin.

> When Geoffrey oversleeps on Groundhog's Day and misses his forecast, nobody in town knows what type of weather to expect.

Informational (Narrative)

Singer, M. (2001). *On the same day in March.* New York: Harperfestival.

> This book explores the weather on a single day in locations around the world.

Informational (Expository)

Weather Watchers series

> These simple informational texts include *It's a Thunderstorm* (Higgins & Ward, 2010) and *It's Hailing* (Higgins, Ward, & Ackerman, 2010). Each book includes

accurate information about these weather patterns, including what they are like and how they form. The books have engaging illustrations and fun facts.

Informational (Expository)

Gibbons, G. (1992). *Weather words and what they mean.* New York: Holiday House.

Using engaging illustrations, this text provides information about key terms related to weather, including temperature, air pressure, moisture, and wind.

Weather Topic Words

air	fog	precipitation	thermometer
blizzard	frost	rain	thunder
breeze	hail	showers	tornado
condensation	haze	sleet	visibility
dew	humidity	slush	water vapor
drizzle	hurricane	snow	weather
drought	lightning	storm	wind chill
flood	meteorologist	sunshine	
flurries	muggy	temperature	

Weather Challenge Words

advisory	environment	measure	pressure
autumn	fair	moisture	season
climate	forecast	observe	speed
conditions	location	partly	
direction	map	predict	

Weather Supportive Words

cold	hot	summer	winter
fall	spring	tools	

Additional Resources

Barrett, J. (1978). *Cloudy with a chance of meatballs.* New York: Athenium Books.
Bauer, M. D. (2011). *In like a lion, out like a lamb.* New York: Holiday House.
Gibbons, G. (1996). *The reasons for seasons.* New York: Holiday House.
Gibbons, G. (2010). *Hurricanes!* New York: Holiday House.
Gibbons, G. (2010). *Tornadoes!* New York: Holiday House.
Rockwell, A. (2008). *Clouds.* New York: Collins.

TOPIC: INSECTS

Concepts

- Insects are living organisms.
- Insects have six legs and three body segments.
- Insects have antennae that they use to smell and feel things.
- Insects grow and change throughout their lives.
- Insects live in certain habitats based on their needs.
- Insects have ways of protecting themselves.

Text Set

Predictable

Carle, E. (1981). *The very hungry caterpillar.* New York: Philomel.

Children are introduced to the life cycle of a butterfly in this children's classic.

Fiction

Poole, A. L. (2000). *The ant and the grasshopper.* New York: Holiday House.

A retelling of an Aesop's fable set in the Imperial Chinese Emperor's Summer Palace. The hard-working ants spend their summer gathering grain for the winter while the grasshopper dances and sings the summer away.

Informational (Narrative)

Krebs, L., & Cis, V. (2008). *The Beeman.* Cambridge, MA: Barefoot Books.

Grandfather is "the Beeman." He teaches his grandson about the lives of bees and how they produce honey. Includes additional information about honeybees in the back of the text.

Informational (Expository)

Micucci, C. (2003). *The life and times of the ant.* Boston: Houghton Mifflin Company.

This book provides engaging information about the life cycle, body parts, and habitats of hard-working ants.

Informational (Expository)

Voak, S. (2009). *Insect detective.* Somerville, MA: Candlewick Press.

There are insects all around, but sometimes you have to know just where to look. Find the different types of insects and learn interesting facts about their lives.

Insects Topic Words

ant	grasshopper	ladybug	praying mantis
bee	honeybee	larva	pupa
butterfly	insect	mosquito	wasp
firefly	katydid	moth	

Insects Challenge Words

abdomen	colony	exoskeleton	pollen
antennae	cooperate	habitat	proboscis
camouflage	defense	larva	protect
chrysalis	mechanism	life-cycle	segment
cocoon	enemy	molt	thorax

Insects Supportive Words

bite	head	legs	wings
eggs	hive	six	
eyes	honey	sting	

Additional Resources

Allen, J., & Humphries, T. (2000). *Are you a bee?* New York: Kingfisher.

Brinkloe, J. (1986). *Fireflies.* New York: Alladin.

Carle, E. (1995). *The very lonely firefly.* New York: Philomel.

Gibbons, G. (1989). *Monarch butterflies.* New York: Holiday House.

Gibbons, G. (2000). *The honeymakers.* New York: HarperCollins.

Glaser, L. (2008). *Dazzling dragonflies: A life cycle story.* Minneapolis, MN: Millbrook Press.

Lawton, C. (2011). *Bugs A to Z.* New York: Scholastic.

Oppenheim, J. (1996). *Have you seen bugs?* New York: Scholastic, Inc.

Rockwell, A. (2001). *Bugs are insects.* New York: HarperCollins Publishers.

TOPIC: HUMAN BODY

Concepts

- **Humans are living organisms.**
- **Human bodies grow and change throughout our lives.**
- **Human bodies have special parts for particular purposes.**
- **Humans live in certain habitats that meet our needs.**

Text Set

Predictable

Lesieg, T. (1999). *The eye book.* New York: Random House.

"My eyes see. His eyes see. I see him. And he sees me." This silly rhyming book helps children to learn about why eyes are such an important body parts.

Fiction

Brown, M. (1979). *Arthur's eyes.* New York: Little Brown and Company.

Arthur has difficulty seeing and needs to get glasses. At first he does not want to wear them, but he soon realizes that they help him to see better and to do his school work.

Informational (Narrative)

Cole, J. (1990). *The magic school bus: Inside the human body.* Logan, IA: Perfection Learning.

When Arnold swallows the magic school bus, the class takes an exciting field trip inside of the human body.

Informational (Expository)

Sweeny, J. (1999). *Me and my amazing body.* New York: Dragonfly Books.

A young girl shows the pictures she has drawn of her body parts and discusses what each part does to keep her healthy.

Informational (Expository)

Ballestrino, P. (1989). *The skeleton inside you.* New York: HarperCollins.

This book provides lots of information about the skeleton and how it helps the body to move and grow.

Human Body Topic Words

abdomen	elbow	ligaments	spine
ankle	eyebrows	lungs	stomach
artery	eyes	mouth	teeth
bones	face	muscle	thigh
brain	foot/feet	nose	torso
cartilage	forehead	organs	vein
cheeks	heart	shoulders	wrist
chest	joints	skeleton	
chin	knees	skin	
ears	legs	skull	

Human Body Challenge Words

adult	movement	oxygen	senses
blood	nourishment	reflex	support
breathe	nutritious	respiration	vision
circulation	organism	rotate	

Human Body Supportive Words

bend	grow	smell	walk
breathe	hear	taste	young
feel	old	touch	

Additional Resources

Aliki. (1989). *My five senses.* New York: Thomas Y. Crowell.
Lesieg, T. (1999). *The nose book.* New York: Random House.
Lyon, G. E. (2010). *The pirate of kindergarten.* New York: Antheneum Books.
Schumaker, B. (2005). *Body parts/Las partes del cuerpo.* Racine, WI: Learning Props.
Taylore, B. (2008). *The best book of the human body.* New York: Kingfisher.

TOPIC: GEOMETRY

Concepts

- Objects in the environment come in different shapes.
- To know the name of a shape, you need to look at the number of its sides, vertices (corners), and surfaces.
- Shapes have the same name whether they are big or small (i.e., size) or turned in a different direction (i.e., orientation) or drawn in a different color.
- Some shapes are two-dimensional and some shapes are three-dimensional.

Text Set

Predictable

Michklethwait, L. (2004). *I spy shapes in art*. New York: Greenwillow Books.

This book asks children to find two- and three-dimensional shapes in famous works of art. Each page begins with the words, "I spy with my little eye."

Fiction

Troiana, J. (2006). *The legend of Spookley the square pumpkin*. New York: Scholastic.

Spookley is different to the other pumpkins because he is square and they are round, but being square helps Spookley to save the day when he blocks a hole in the fence and prevents the other pumpkins from rolling down the hill.

Informational (Narrative)

Burns, M. (1994). *The greedy triangle*. New York: Scholastic.

The greedy triangle thinks his life would be more interesting as another shape, so he tries becoming a quadrilateral, a pentagon, a hexagon, and many other shapes before deciding he likes being a triangle best of all.

Informational (Narrative)

Neushwander, C. (2005). *Mummy math: An adventure in geometry*. New York: Square Fish.

Two children must use their knowledge about geometric solids to solve clues and find their way out of a pyramid.

Informational (Expository)

The Metropolitan Museum of Art. (2005). *Museum shapes*. New York: Little Brown and Company.

Find and label shapes in great works of art from the museum's collection.

Geometry Topic Words

angle	line	pyramid	sphere
circle	octagon	quadrilateral	square
cone	parallelogram	quarter-circle	trapezoid
corner	pentagon	rectangle	triangle
cube	plane	rhombus	vertices
cylinder	point	semi-circle	
half-circle	polygon	shape	
hexagon	prism	side	

Geometry Challenge Words

center	equal	perimeter	symmetry
circumference	flat	perpendicular	three-dimensional
closed	geometry	plane	two-dimensional
compass	length	solid	
diagonal	parallel	surface	

Geometry Supportive Words

draw	four	round	three
five	picture	straight	two

Additional Resources

Blackstone, S., & Bell, S. (2006). *Ship shapes*. Cambridge, MA: Barefoot Books.

Falwell, C. (2007). *Shape capers*. New York: Greenwillow.

Hall, M. (2011). *Perfect square*. New York: Greenwillow.

Hoban, T. (2000). *Cubes, cones, cylinders, & spheres*. New York: Greenwillow.

Maradu, T. (1996). *Line and circle*. Chennai, India: Tulika Publishers.

Murphy, S. J. (2001). *Captain Invincible and the space shapes*. New York: HarperCollins.

Schoonmaker, E. (2011). *Square cat*. New York: Alladin.

Walsh, E. S. (2007). *Mouse shapes*. New York: Harcourt.

TOPIC: TRANSPORTATION

Concepts

- Transportation is how people and products move from one place to another.
- Throughout history, people have used different modes of transportation.
- Different modes of transportation have different uses as well as advantages and disadvantages.
- People use private vehicles and public systems to reach their destinations.

Text Set

Predictable

Mayo, M., & Ayliffe, A. (2004) *Choo choo clickety-clack.* Minneapolis, MN: Carolrhoda Books.

> This book explores different uses of modes of transportation as well as the noises they make. Each page ends with the predictable refrain, "Off they go."

Fiction

Piper, W. (2007). *The Little Engine That Could.* New York: Grosset & Dunlap.

> Even though he is small, the determined engine transports his cargo of toys over the mountain to the children who are awaiting its arrival.

Informational (Narrative)

Scarry, R. (1974). *Richard Scarry's cars trucks and things that go.* New York: Golden Books.

> Explore every type of vehicle imaginable when the Pig family goes on a picnic.

Informational (Narrative)

Baer, E. (1990). *This is the way we go to school: A book about children around the world.* New York: Scholastic.

> Children around the world describe the mode of transportation they use to get to school.

Informational Text (Expository)

DK Publishing. (1994). *Big book of things that go.* New York: Author.

> With engaging pictures and information, this book helps children to understand why different types of vehicles are useful.

Transportation Topic Words

airplane	convertible	hot air	sail	tricycle
axle	donkey	balloons	ship	truck
bicycle	driver	jet	shuttle	van
boat	engine	limousine	spaceship	vehicle
buggy	ferry	motorcycle	steam	wagon
bus	helicopter	pilot	subway	wheel
cab	highway	plane	taxi	
cart	horse	rocket	train	

Transportation Challenge Words

cargo	distance	goods	product	steam
coal	energy	lumber	public	transport
community	fare	mile	route	transportation
delivery	freight	mode	speed	travel
destination	gasoline	private	station	

Transportation Supportive Words

drive	home	run	traffic
fast	move	slow	walk

Additional Resources

Crews, D. (1992). *Freight train*. New York: Greenwillow Books.

Downs, M. (2003). *The noisy airplane ride*. Berkeley, CA: Tricycle Press.

DK Publishing. (1998) *Big book of trains*. New York: Author.

Konrad, M. S. (2009). *Getting there*. Toronto: Tundra Books.

Mitton, T., & Parker, A. (2005). *Cool cars*. Boston: Kingfisher.

Nelson, R. (2003). *Transportation then and now*. Minneapolis, MN: Lerner Publications.

Slaughter, T. (2012). *Boat works*. Maplewood, NJ: Blue Apple Books.

Walker, S. M., & Feldmann, R. (2001). *Wheels and axles*. Minneapolis, MN: Lerner Publications.

TOPIC: CAREERS

Concepts

- **Members of a community have needs and responsibilities.**
- **Adults do work that is important to meet the community's needs.**
- **There are many different types of jobs/careers that help to meet the needs of the community.**

Text Set

Predictable

Hallinan, P. K. (2006). *When I grow up.* Nashville, TN: Candy Cane Press.

In this delightful rhyming book, children imagine all of the careers they could have when they grow up. There is one job listed for each letter of the alphabet, beginning with actor, baker, carpenter, dancer, and engineer.

Fiction

Huneck, S. (2008). *Sally gets a job.* New York: Abrams Books.

Sally, the family dog, considers jobs she might do so she will not be lonely when her family goes off to school and work.

Informational (Narrative)

Rockwell, A. (2000). *Career day.* New York: HarperCollins.

On Career Day at school, the children introduce special visitors and the class learns about the different work that people do.

Informational Text (Narrative)

Caseley, J. (2002) *On the town: A community adventure.* New York: Greenwillow.

For homework, the teacher gives Charlie a notebook where he can draw and write about the people and places in his community.

Informational Text (Expository)

DK Publishing. (2001). *Jobs people do.* New York: Author.

Each page provides information about a different trade or profession with facts about tools, equipment, and the workplace.

Careers Topic Words

ambulance	crossing guard	lifeguard	president
archaeologist	dentist	mayor	professor
architect	doctor	member	repairman
career	engineer	neighbor	responsible
chef	farmer	nurse	secretary
construction worker	firefighter	paleontologist	teacher
	hospital	park ranger	waiter
counselor	librarian	police officer	

Careers Challenge Words

adult	community	income	safety
career	cooperation	government	transportation
citizen	education	laws	
city	employee	professional	
common	health	responsibility	

Careers Supportive Words

boss	job	need	work
helper	money	school	worker

Additional Resources

Cooper Katz, S. (2007). *Whose hat is this?* Mankato, MN: Picture Window Books.
Cooper Katz, S. (2007). *Whose tools are these?* Mankato, MN: Picture Window Books.
Cooper Katz, S. (2007). *Whose vehicle is this?* Mankato, MN: Picture Window Books.
Leake, D. (2008). *People in the community series.* Mankato, MN: Heinemann-Raintree.
Ready D. (2006). *Community helpers series.* North Mankato, MN: Capstone Press.
Scarry, R. (1968). *What people do all day.* New York: Random House.

APPENDIX B

Examples of Vocabulary Terms Children Should Know, PreK–Grade 2

MATHEMATICS

above	create	identify	proportion
addition	cube	inch	rectangle
analyze	cylinder	length	ruler
behind	data	lower	season
below	describe	mile	sequence
between	difference	multiplication	shape
calendar	division	next to	similar
category	equation	number (and	sphere
circle	estimate	number words)	square
classify	explanation	operations	subtraction
compare	feet	outcome	temperature
contrast	height	over	weather
compose	hexagon	pattern	
cone	higher	predict	

SCIENCE

adapt	climate	distance	evaporation
animal	color	duration	explore
brain	conclude	earth	extinct
breathe	cooperate	electricity	graph
carbon dioxide	creature	energy	gravity
characteristic	density	environment	habitat
classify	discover	evaluate	heart

inquiry	marine	protection	sort
insect	movement	question	sound
investigate	nourish	reason	stem
life cycle	nutrition	reflect	survival
light	observe	reproduction	temperature
liquid	ocean	root	test
location	organism	science	tide
lungs	organs	scientist	warm-blooded
machine	oxygen	senses	weather
magnet	photosynthesis	shadow	weight
magnify	plant	shape	
mammal	predator	solution	

LITERATURE AND LANGUAGE ARTS

antonym	dialogue	illustrator	quotation marks
appendix	dictionary	imagination	resolution
argument	discussion	index	response
audience	elaborate	inference	retelling
author	emotion	information book	rhyme
autobiography	episode	interpretation	setting
biography	evidence	introduction	shared reading/ writing
capital letter	exclamation mark	main idea	storybook
chapter	extension	mystery	strategy
chapter book	fairy tale	nonfiction	summarize
characters	folk tale	paragraph	synonym
comma	fiction	period	table of contents
comprehension	generalization	plot	title
conclusion	genre	poem	title page
copyright	glossary	predictable book	topic sentence
definition	graph	prediction	vocabulary
description	illustrations	question	voice
diagram			

SOCIAL STUDIES

Abraham Lincoln

American Indian

ballot

Benjamin Franklin

calendar

cause

celebration

ceremony

Christopher Columbus

city

community

Congress

constitution

country

courage

culture

customs

decade

Declaration of Independence

democracy

east

effect

fire fighter

flag

future

geography

George Washington

globe

government

hero

history

holiday

honesty

independence

justice

law

leader

left

legend

library

location

map

Martin Luther King

month

mountain

north

ocean

past

patriotism

Pledge of allegiance

police officer

post officer

present

responsibility

revolution

right

scale

south

state

Statue of liberty

Thanksgiving

Thomas Jefferson

town

traditions

traffic

United States of America

vote

west

year

HEALTH

beans

blood

bones

butter

calories

carbohydrates

cereal

climbing

dairy

dentist

diet

doctor

eggs

energy

exercise

fats

fever

fiber

fitness

fresh

fruit

grains

healthy

heart rate

ingredients

iron

jogging

jumping

meat

minerals

muscles

nourishment

nutrition

nuts

oats

physical activity

protein	skipping	temperature	yogurt
rice	spinach	weight	
riding	strengthen	wheat	
running	stretching	vegetable	

ARTS

actor/actress	drama	mystery	setting
artist	easel	performer	stage
audience	entertain	pitch	story
cast	expression	production	superhero
comedy	film	props	texture
costumes	makeup	rhythm	theater
dance	melody	role	tragedy
design	movie	scale	video
dialogue	music	script	voice

References

Beck, I., & McKeown, M. (2007). Increasing young low-income children's oral vocabulary repertoires through rich and focused instruction. *Elementary School Journal, 107*(3), 251–271.

Beck, I., McKeown, M., & Kucan, L. (2002). *Bringing words to life.* New York: Guilford.

Biemiller, A., & Boote, C. (2006). An effective method for building meaning vocabulary in primary grades. *Journal of Educational Psychology, 98*(1), 44–62.

Billman, A. K., Duke, N. K., Hilden, K. R., Zhang, S., Roberts, K., Halladay, J. L., Martin, N. M., & Schaal, A. M. (2008). *Concepts of Comprehension Assessment (COCA)*. Retrieved from http://msularc.educ.msu.edu/what-we-do/projects/mai-coca/

Bishop, D., & Adams, C. (1990). A prospective study of the relationship between specific language impairment, phonological disorders and reading retardation. *Journal of Child Psychology and Psychiatry and Allied Disciplines, 31*(7), 1027–1050.

Bloom, P. (2000). *How children learn the meanings of words.* Cambridge, MA: MIT Press.

Bowman, B., Donovan, S., & Burns, M. S. (2000). *Eager to learn: Educating our preschoolers.* Washington, DC: National Academy Press.

Bruner, J., Olver, R. R., & Greenfield, P. M. (1966). *Studies in cognitive growth.* New York: Wiley.

Bus, A., & Van Ijzendoorn, M. (1995). Mothers reading to their 3-year-olds: The role of mother-child attachment security in becoming literate. *Reading Research Quarterly, 30*(4), 998–1015.

Carey, S., & Bartlett, E. (1978). Acquiring a single new word. *Papers and Reports on Child Language Development, 15*, 17–29.

Carle, E. (1981). *The very hungry caterpillar.* New York: Philomel.

Carle, E. (1987). *The tiny seed.* New York: Little Simon.

Carle, E. (1996). *The grouchy ladybug.* New York: HarperCollins.

Cherry, L. (2003). *How groundhog's garden grew.* New York: Blue Sky Press.

Clark, R., Kirschner, P., & Sweller, J. (2012). Putting students on the path to learning. *American Educator, 36*(1), 6–11.

Coleman, D., & Pimentel, S. (2012). *Revised publishers' criteria for the Common Core State Standards in English Language Arts and Literacy, K–2; Grades 3–12.* Washington, DC: National Governor's Association.

Coyne, M., McCoach, B., & Kapp, S. (2007). Vocabulary intervention for kindergarten students: Comparing extended instruction and incidental exposure. *Learning Disability Quarterly, 30*(2), 74–88.

DiSalvo-Ryan, D. (1994). *City green.* New York: HarperCollins.

Duckworth, E. (2006). *"The having of wonderful ideas"* and other essays on teaching and learning (3rd Ed.). New York: Teachers College Press.

Duke, N. K. (2000). 3.6 minutes per day: The scarcity of informational texts in first grade. *Reading Research Quarterly, 35*(2), 202–224.

Duke, N. K., & Kays, J. (1998). "Can I say 'once upon a time'?" Kindergarten children developing knowledge of information book language. *Early Childhood Research Quarterly, 13,* 295–318.

Elleman, A., Lindo, E., Morphy, P., & Compton, D. (2009). The impact of vocabulary instruction on passage-level comprehension of school-age children: A meta-analysis. *Journal of Educational Effectiveness, 2*(1), 1–44.

Engelbert, P. (2009). From the big bang to the big crunch. In P. Engelbert (Ed.), *Space probe: Astronomy & space.* Farmington Hills, MI: Gale Cengage Learning.

Farkas, G., & Beron, K. (2004). The detailed age trajectory of oral vocabulary knowledge: Differences by class and race. *Social Science Research, 33*(3), 464–497.

Freeman, D. (1976). *Corduroy.* New York: Puffin.

Goodman, E. (2009). *Plant secrets.* Watertown, MA: Charlesbridge Publishing.

Gopnik, A., Meltzoff, A., & Kuhl, P. (1999). *The scientist in the crib.* New York: William Morrow.

Graves, M. (2006). *The vocabulary book.* New York: Teachers College Press.

Harris, J., Golinkoff, R., & Hirsh-Pasek, K. (2011). Lessons from the crib for the classroom: How children really learn vocabulary. In S. B. Neuman & D. Dickinson (Eds.), *Handbook on early literacy research* (Vol. III, pp. 49–65). New York: Guilford.

Hart, B., & Risley, T. (1995). *Meaningful differences.* Baltimore, MD: Brookes.

Hart, B., & Risley, T. (2003). The early catastrophe. *American Educator, 27*(4),6–9.

Hirsch, E. D. (2003). Reading comprehension requires knowledge of words and the world. *American Educator, 27*(10), 1316–1322, 1328–1329, 1348.

Holdaway, D. (1979). *The foundations of literacy.* Portsmouth, NH: Heinemann.

Juel, C., Biancarosa, G., Coker, D., & Deffes, R. (2003, April). Walking with Rosie: A cautionary tale of early reading instruction. *Educational Leadership,* 12–18.

Kaefer, T., & Neuman, S. B. (2011). A bi-directional relationship between conceptual organization and word learning. Paper presented at the annual meeting of the Literacy Research Association, Jacksonville, FL.

Kegal, C., Bus, A., & IJzendoorn, M. (2011). Differential susceptibility in early literacy instruction through computer games. *Mind, Brain and Education, 5*(2), 71–78.

Kimmel, E., & Huling, P. (2004). *Cactus soup.* Tarrytown, NY: Marshall Cavendish.

Martin, B., & Archambault, J. (1991). *Chicka chicka boom boom.* New York: Little & Simon.

Marulis, L. M., & Neuman, S. B. (2010). The effects of vocabulary training on word learning: A meta-analysis. *Review of Educational Research, 80*(3), 300–335.

Marulis, L. M., & Neuman, S. B. (in press). How vocabulary interventions affect children at risk: A meta-analytic review. *Journal of Educational Effectiveness.*

Marzano, R. (2004). *Building background knowledge for academic achievement.* Alexandria, VA: Association for Supervision and Curriculum Development.

McDermott, G. (1972). *Anansi the spider.* New York: Henry Holt & Company.

McDermott, G. (1993). *Anansi the spider*. New York: Scholastic.

McMurray, B. (2007). Defusing the childhood vocabulary explosion. *Science, 1126.*

Micucci, C. (2006). *The life and times of the ant.* New York: Houghton Mifflin Harcourt.

Mol, S., Bus, A., & deJong, M. (2009). Interactive book reading in early education: A tool to stimulate print knowledge as well as oral language. *Review of Educational Research, 79*(2), 979–1007.

Mol, S., Bus, A., deJong, M., & Smeets, D. (2008). Added value of dialogic parent-child book readings: A meta-analysis. *Early Education and Development, 19*(1), 7–26.

Mol, S., & Neuman, S. B. (2012). *Sharing information books with kindergartners: The role of parents' extratextual talk and socioeconomic status.* Ann Arbor: University of Michigan.

Monks, L. (2007). *Aaaarrgghh! Spider!* New York: Houghton Mifflin Harcourt.

Morrow, L. M. (1988). Young children's responses to one-to-one readings in school settings. *Reading Research Quarterly, 23*(1), 89–107.

Nagy, W., Anderson, R. C., & Herman, P. (1987). Learning word meanings from context during normal reading. *American Educational Research Journal, 24,* 237–270.

Nagy, W., & Scott, J. (2000). Vocabulary processes. In M. Kamil, P. Mosenthal, P. Pearson, & R. Barr (Eds.), *Handbook of reading research* (Volume III, pp. 269–284). Mahwah, NJ: Erlbaum.

National Early Literacy Panel. (2008). *Developing early literacy.* Washington, DC: National Institute for Literacy.

Neuman, S. B., Copple, C., & Bredekamp, S. (2000). *Learning to read and write: Developmentally appropriate practice.* Washington, DC: National Association for the Education of Young Children.

Neuman, S. B., & Dwyer, J. (2009). Missing in action: Vocabulary instruction in pre-K. *The Reading Teacher, 62,* 384–392.

Neuman, S. B., Dwyer, J., Koh, S., & Wright, T. (2007). *The world of words: A vocabulary intervention for preschool children.* Ann Arbor, MI: University of Michigan.

Neuman, S. B., & Gallagher, P. (1994). Joining together in literacy learning: Teenage mothers and children. *Reading Research Quarterly, 29*(4), 382–401.

Neuman, S. B., Newman, E., & Dwyer, J. (2011). Educational effects of a vocabulary intervention on preschoolers' word knowledge and conceptual development: A cluster randomized trial. *Reading Research Quarterly, 46*(3), 249–272.

Neuman, S. B., & Roskos, K. (2012). Helping children become knowledgeable through text. *Reading Teacher, 3,* 207–210.

Oppenheim, J. (1996). *Have you seen bugs?* New York: Scholastic.

Pappas, C. (1991). Young children's strategies in learning the "book language" of information books. *Discourse Processes, 14*(2), 203–225.

Pearson, P. D., Hiebert, E., & Kamil, M. (2007). Vocabulary assessment: What we know and what we need to learn. *Reading Research Quarterly, 42*(2), 282–296.

Pinkham, A., Neuman, S. B., & Lillard, A. (2011, November). You can say that again! Preschoolers need repeated exposures to gain expressive vocabulary. Paper presented at the annual meeting of the Literacy Research Association, Jacksonville, FL.

Pollard-Durodola, S., Gonzalez, J., Simmons, D., Davis, M., Simmons, D., & Nava-Walichowski, M. (2012). Using knowledge networks to develop preschoolers' content vocabulary. *The Reading Teacher, 65*(4), 265–274.

Price, L., Bradley, B., & Smith, J. (2012). A comparison of preschool teachers' talk during storybook and information book read-alouds. *Early Childhood Research Quarterly, 27*(3), 426–440.

Price, L., van Kleeck, A., & Huberty, C. (2009). Talk during book sharing between parents and preschool children: A comparison between storybook and expository book conditions. *Reading Research Quarterly, 44*(2), 171–194.

Rice, N. (1980). *Cognition to language.* Baltimore, MD: University Park Press.

Rodriquez, E., & Tamis-LeMonda, C. (2011). Trajectories of the home learning environment across the first 5 years: Associations with children's vocabulary and literacy skills at prekindergarten. *Child Development, 82*(4), 1058–1075.

Scott, J., & Nagy, W. (2004). Developing word consciousness. In J. F. Baumann & E. Kame'enui (Eds.), *Vocabulary instruction: Research to practice* (pp. 201–217). New York: Guilford.

Silverman, R. (2007). A comparison of three methods of vocabulary instruction during read-alouds in kindergarten. *Elementary School Journal, 108*(2), 97–113.

Silverman, R., & Hines, S. (2009). The effects of multimedia-enhanced instruction on the English-language learners and non-English language pre-kindergarten through second grade. *Journal of Educational Psychology, 101*(2), 305–314.

Stahl, S., & Nagy, W. (2006). *Teaching word meanings.* Mahwah, NJ: Erlbaum.

Stanovich, K., & Cunningham, A. (1992). Studying the consequences of literacy within a literate society: The cognitive correlates of print exposure. *Memory & Cognition, 20*(1), 51–68.

Weizman, Z. O., & Snow, C. E. (2001). Lexical input as related to children's vocabulary acquisition: Effects of sophisticated exposure and support for meaning. *Developmental Psychology, 37*(2), 265–279.

Wesche, M., & Paribakt, T. (1996). Assessing second language vocabulary knowledge: Depth versus breadth. *Canadian Modern Language Review, 53*(1), 13–40.

Wright, T., & Neuman, S. B. (December, 2009). What classroom observations reveal about vocabulary instruction: A study of 55 kindergarten classrooms. Paper presented at the annual meeting of the Literacy Reading Conference/National Reading Conference, Albuquerque, NM.

Wright, T., & Neuman, S. B. (in press). *Vocabulary instruction in commonly used kindergarten core reading curricula. The Elementary School Journal.*

Index

About the Author

Susan B. Neuman is a professor in Teaching and Learning at the University of Michigan and New York University specializing in early literacy development. Previously, she has served as the U.S. Assistant Secretary for Elementary and Secondary Education. In her role as Assistant Secretary, she established the Early Reading First program, developed the Early Childhood Educator Professional Development Program, and was responsible for all activities in Title I of the Elementary and Secondary Act. She has served on the IRA Board of Directors (2001–2003), and other numerous boards of nonprofit organizations. She is currently the co-editor of *Reading Research Quarterly*, the most prestigious journal in reading research. Her research and teaching interests include early childhood policy, curriculum, and early reading instruction, preK-grade 3, for children who live in poverty. She has written over 100 articles and authored and edited 11 books, including the *Handbook of Early Literacy Research* (Volumes I, II, III) with David Dickinson, *Changing the Odds for Children at Risk* (Teachers College Press, 2009), *Educating the Other America* (2008), and *Multimedia and Literacy Development* (2008). Her most recent book is *Giving Our Children a Fighting Chance: Poverty, Literacy, and the Development of Information Capital* (Teachers College Press, 2012).

Tanya S. Wright is an assistant professor of language and literacy in the department of Teacher Education and a principal investigator for the Literacy Achievement Research Center at Michigan State University. She is the winner of the 2012 Outstanding Dissertation of the Year Award from the International Reading Association. She is a former kindergarten teacher whose research focuses on curriculum and instruction in early language and literacy, with a particular interest in improving educational outcomes for children living in poverty. Her recent work concentrates on the roles of teachers and curricular materials in promoting oral language, vocabulary, and background knowledge development for young children. Wright received her Ph.D. with a specialization in language, literacy, and culture from the University of Michigan, her M.A. from the reading specialist program at Teachers College, Columbia University, and her B.A. in anthropology from Columbia University.